# Office Collectibles

*100 Years of Business Technology*

Thomas A. Russo

*Schiffer Publishing Ltd*

4880 Lower Valley Road, Atglen, PA 19310 USA

# ACKNOWLEDGMENTS

This book might not have been published without the help of my wife, Mary Jo, who made the initial contact with the Schiffer Publishing Company. For over 46 years, she and my children have been supportive of my endeavors. I cannot imagine having made that journey without her and the family.

I would also like to thank my fellow collectors, who have willingly shared information, books, articles and industry ephemera with me.

Nina Wolf, a respected photographer from Cleveland, Ohio, took the photographs that are of a better quality.

A special thanks to a long time friend, David P. Sheridan, who gave me copies of the "Remington Notes" volumes 1, 2, 3, 4, and 5, for research information.

Also, three wonderful quarterly newsletters that I have referred to for research and accuracy checks: "ETCetera" by Darryl Rehr; "Typewriter Exchange" by Michael A. Brown; and, "Ribbon Tin News" by Hobart D. Van Deusen.

And, finally, I would like to thank my long time friend and associate, Sonya Zawalski, who has typed, edited and offered formatting advice concerning this book

**Library of Congress Cataloging-in-Publication Data**

Russo, Thomas A.
    Office collectibles: 100 years of business technology/
    Thomas A. Russo.
       p. cm.
    ISBN: 0-7643-1177-8
    1. Office equipment and supplies. I. Title.
    HF5521 .R87  2000
    651'.2'075--dc21            00-009477

Designed by "Sue"
Type set in Dutch809 BT
ISBN: 0-7643-1177-8
Printed in China
1 2 3 4

Published by Schiffer Publishing Ltd.
4880 Lower Valley Road
Atglen, PA 19310
Phone: (610) 593-1777; Fax: (610) 593-2002
E-mail: Schifferbk@aol.com
Please visit our web site catalog at
**www.schifferbooks.com**

This book may be purchased from the publisher.
Include $3.95 for shipping.
Please try your bookstore first.
We are interested in hearing from authors
with book ideas on related subjects.
You may write for a free catalog.

In Europe, Schiffer books are distributed by
Bushwood Books
6 Marksbury Ave.
Kew Gardens
Surrey TW9 4JF England
Phone: 44 (0) 208 392-8585; Fax: 44 (0) 208 392-9876
E-mail: Bushwd@aol.com
Free postage in the U.K., Europe; air mail at cost.

# CONTENTS

One of eleven aisles of the Thomas A. Russo Collection

4

# INTRODUCTION

The artifacts and nostalgia displayed in the following chapters are a result of the author's unending search for antique miscellaneous office technologies and after-products. His search began in 1987 and continues through the present day. Antique typewriters, adding machines and calculators are the main part of his collection. Some of them are described and/or pictured in this book, but the emphasis in the following chapters is on "diversity." The intention is to give the reader a glimpse of the many after-market products the office equipment and systems industry spawned. It is impossible to visit an antique marketplace and not see a remnant of this great after-market, "Miscellaneous Office Technologies."

No one knows exactly when the "office" began, but we are reasonably certain that communications or writing and counting played a major role in the business that was conducted in those first offices.

Communication or writing probably had its beginning prior to 3600 BC. About that time Egypt and Sumeria were using a system of thought pictures called "hieroglyphics." Over a period of time, this system was broken down into "syllabaries" or collections of signs depicting different syllables; and finally a further development occurred that produced signs to indicate initial sounds and hence became letters. Examples of this alphabetic writing date back to 3000 BC in Egypt. Later, during the time of Homer, the Greeks adapted and further developed the "Allied Aramaic" system and began calling its components by the Semitic names that included the first and second letters, "Alphabeta" from the Hebrew "Aleph, Beth" or the Arabic "Alif, ba."

Ancient hieroglyphics were scribed in stone. Expanding use of the alphabet created a need for a more portable substance on which to write. Egypt is credited with the production of paper. They used the stem of the papyrus plant, which was found to grow in abundance along the Nile River. Strips were placed vertically and horizontally on top of one another and pressed into a sheet. The durability of these sheets of papyrus paper is acknowledged by the fact that after the passing of 5,000 years, some are still in existence today.

Black ink was created by mixing soot with water and vegetable gums on a wooden palette. A simple reed, pointed at the tip, served as a pen. Later many attempts were made to perfect the pen. Below are examples of some of these early devices.

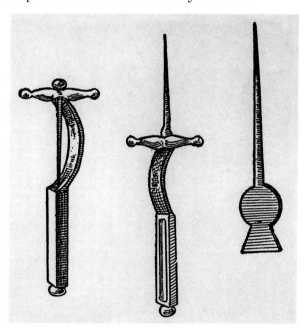

Early writing implements

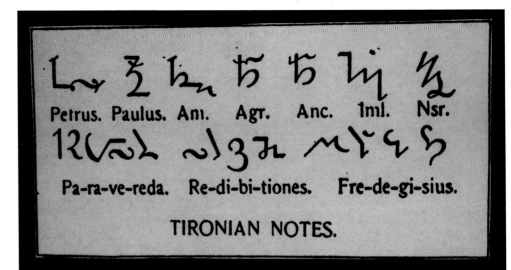

Tironian Shorthand

Petrus. Paulus. Ani. Agr. Anc. Iml. Nsr.

Pa-ra-ve-reda. Re-di-bi-tiones. Fre-de-gi-sius.

TIRONIAN NOTES.

And there you have it, the rudiments of the tools for the early office: the alphabet, paper, ink and the pen. Forms of these inventions are still with us today. But writing with paper, pen and ink was laborious and often messy. A better "system" was needed. A system that would "save time."

Marcus Tullius Tiro invented just such a system in 63 BC. It was in cursive longhand and used many abbreviations. It came to be taught in Roman schools and was used to record speeches and to transcribe correspondence. Roman Emperors Julius Caesar and Augustus were said to have been skilled in using this initial form of "shorthand." Above is an example of Tiro's system of shorthand.

The quest for writing speed did not end with Tiro's system, although it was many centuries before the idea was revised and further developed. In 1588, an Englishman, Timothy Bright, M.D. (1551-1615), published "Characterie," a publication describing the "nature and objects of his shorthand system." At least eight other men are credited with refining and developing a system of shorthand between 1588 to 1837. The chart at right illustrates some of the similarities and/or differences in the various shorthand systems.

| | Bright 1588 | Willis 1602 | Rich 1644 | Mason 1707 | Gurney 1752 | Byrom 1767 | Taylor 1786 | Moore 1799 | Pitman 1837 |
|---|---|---|---|---|---|---|---|---|---|
| A | | | | | | | | | |
| B | | | | | | | | | |
| C | | | | | | | | | |
| D | | | | | | | | | |
| E | | | | | | | | | |
| F | | | | | | | | | |
| G | | | | | | | | | |
| H | | | | | | | | | |
| I | | | | | | | | | |
| J | | | | | | | | | |
| K | | | | | | | | | |
| L | | | | | | | | | |
| M | | | | | | | | | |
| N | | | | | | | | | |
| O | | | | | | | | | |
| P | | | | | | | | | |
| Q | | | | | | | | | |
| R | | | | | | | | | |
| S | | | | | | | | | |
| T | | | | | | | | | |
| U | | | | | | | | | |
| V | | | | | | | | | |
| W | | | | | | | | | |
| X | | | | | | | | | |
| Y | | | | | | | | | |
| Z | | | | | | | | | |
| Ch | | | | | | | | | |
| Sh | | | | | | | | | |
| Th | | | | | | | | | |

FROM NEW INTERNATIONAL ENCYCLOPÆDIA
Copyright by Dodd, Mead & Co.

The alphabet compared to eight shorthand systems.

The last system in the preceding illustration was invented by Sir Isaac Pitman (1813-1897), also known as the inventor of phonography. On November 15, 1837, Pitman's book *Stenographic Sound Hand* made its first appearance. By the year 1889, approximately 97 percent of shorthand writers in American offices used the Pitman method.

Finally, in 1888, John Robert Gregg, an Irish stenographer, invented a markedly different shorthand system which combined commonly used letters into brief forms to speed up the process. The Gregg system was introduced in 1893 and quickly became the shorthand system used by 90 percent of the shorthand Instructors.

The many refinements and inventions of shorthand systems were perhaps bellwethers leading the revolution in offices throughout the world. "Speed" was the motivating force that would dominate the rapid progress in the office.

The adding machine, calculator, typewriter, dictating machine and copier were some of the early mechanical inventions that would power that progress.

Perhaps the typewriter, more than any other office product, best demonstrates the mechanical ingenuity of the times. Many regard Christopher Latham Sholes as the father of the typewriter.

Sir Isaac Pitman

Christopher
Latham Sholes

Sholes & Glidden Typewriter

Sholes and Carlos Glidden invented and patented their first typewriter in 1868, but it was not introduced until 1873, when it was manufactured by the E. Remington & Sons Company of Ilion, New York.

There were typewriters before the Sholes or Remington typewriters, but none of these early attempts was practical. An operator could not attain speeds that would allow typing substantially faster than writing. The Remington did! In 1853, the handwriting speed record was 30 words per minute. Early Remington advertisements stated the typewriter was three times faster than the pen. The Remington proved to be even faster. Remington typewriter sales eventually were so successful that by 1906 Remington factories were producing "a typewriter a minute" to meet the demand.

This was a remarkable achievement considering that a typewriter had hundreds of small and minute parts that must work in unison to create a perfectly aligned typewritten document.

By the 1880s and 1890s, the office began another dramatic change. Women proved to be very proficient as typewriter operators. In fact, these women came to be called "Typewriters," a source of many jokes during that period. Economically, women could also be hired for a fraction of the cost of men. As a result, the office that once was dominated by male secretaries almost overnight changed to offices dominated by women in secretarial positions.

Remington Typewriter Company advertisement

Male secretaries

Women secretaries

Telephone Company Office
with women employees

Combined office–men and
women working together

Male-dominated Russian office.

Above right:
Count Tolstoy with his "three"
assistants in his small "home" office

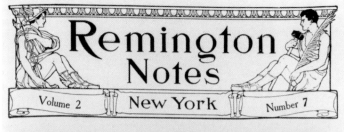

Typists became faster and faster. Speed contests were held in which typists competed using equipment supplied by various manufacturers. One such typist was Mary E. Orr. Miss Orr was a former school teacher who began a new career as a "copyist." Her job was to duplicate documents by typing them over for a file copy. After starting her own business, she began entering typing speed contests during her spare time. Her skills were honed to the point where she achieved a record of 98.7 words per minute and sustained it for ten minutes.

She was hired by the Remington Company and proved herself to be indispensable. In 1907, she became a member of the Board of Directors of the Remington Typewriter Company, the first woman to hold such a position with a major corporation.

Miss Mary E. Orr

It soon became apparent that 98.7 words per minute did not satisfy the office quest for speed. In 1912, the Hooven Automatic Typewriter was invented. A perforator punched holes in a roll of paper and the roll was then placed on a player device that was attached to a typewriter. The Hooven operated in a fashion similar to a player piano. Letters could now be typed over and over at high speed without the help of several typists.

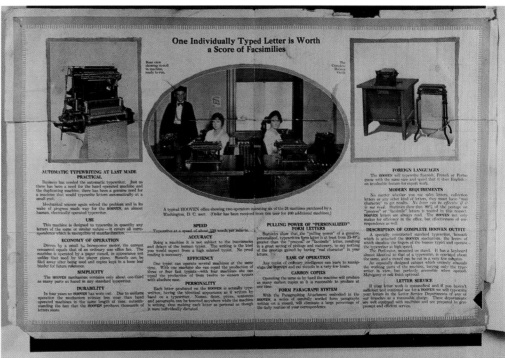

Above and right:
Hooven Automatic Typewriter
Brochure

Soon the Hooven technology gave way to paper tape (5 and 8 channel tape). In the late 1950s, Remington Rand introduced a paper tape automatic electric typewriter called the "Synchro-tape Automatic Typewriter."

It produced automatic machine-to-machine processing with instantaneous wire transmission of written records between all locations. It used punched paper tape that would perfectly control the writing of sales orders, shipping papers, invoices and automatic conversion of data to punched cards.

Synchro-tape Automatic Typewriter,
*Fortune Magazine*, July 1959

## FASTER–FASTER–FASTER

During the late 1950s, IBM introduced an automatic typewriter that was capable of storing information on a magnetic tape. It was initially used for repetitive letters, but a German IBM branch office found that it also facilitated the editing of a document and coined a new phrase, "word processing." As a result repetitive typing became a by-product and the main application was developed around the ability to make extensive editing changes without manually retyping the entire document. Then came magnetic card, followed by floppy disks, and then random access memory (RAM). Word processing was the application that ushered in the new era of the desktop computers, where the ultimate goal of "voice recognition" has finally been achieved. One may now, simply talk to a computer and it will automatically store that conversation and print it upon demand.

All this was achieved during the 127 years since 1873. The QWERTY keyboard that originally appeared on the first Sholes & Glidden typewriter made the transition easily and is on all modern desktop computers. It stands as a reminder of the tremendous office evolution that has transpired. The adding machine, calculator, copier and dictating machines developed along similar lines to achieve the same end as integral parts of today's computers.

All of these ingenious "time saving" inventions are a wonderful part of the history of the office. As such they will remain treasures to collect, preserve and display.

Since most of the items pictured in this book were actually purchased by the author, the prices he paid was a primary consideration in the valuing process for each item, but not the only factor. He also used his experience in tracking auction prices, private sales and the Internet. However, the true value is really based on how badly the seller wants to sell; and how anxious the buyer is to buy. Finally, condition and appearance are important in most sales. If parts are missing, restoration can cost thousands of dollars and may in fact dwarf the value of the machine.

Collecting and preserving a small part of this glorious history has been especially gratifying to the author since he has been an eyewitness to a big part of this wonderful period in the office revolution.

# CHAPTER I
# ADDING MACHINES AND CALCULATORS

No one really knows when humans first began to count. Historians believe that it was probably when they first began to communicate. In the beginning, fingers were used to count and since there were only ten fingers, the decimal system of base ten was developed.

The Babylonians developed the number twelve, which led to the duo decimal system. Some historians believe that this was probably due to the fact that there were twelve full moons in a year.

Early cuneiform inscriptions that originated about 2200 B.C., tell us that the Babylonians invented what might have been the first adding machine. It could be described as a rectangular board with ruled lines on the surface. Pebbles were placed at various locations to represent different values. About 800 A.D. the Chinese became the first to use the zero (0), however, the first record of a zero appearing was in an Arabic document about 873 A.D.

A discovery that enabled the world to frame a system of mathematics containing whole numbers and fractions proved to be the decimal notation. It did not surface until 1617 A.D., when John Napier of England first discovered and pioneered its use.

William Schikard, in 1622 A.D., is credited with being the first individual to develop a calculator that could perform multiple functions, i.e. add, subtract, multiply and divide. However, no actual machine, prototype or otherwise, has ever been discovered. Only his drawings attest to his creation.

The first surviving truly mechanical calculator was the invention of Blaise Pascal in 1642 A.D. It is the writer's opinion that it was very appropriate to later name a computer programming language, Pascal, after this illustrious inventor.

Finally, in 1820, a Frenchman, Charles Xavier Thomas of Colmar, France, invented and successfully manufactured a mechanical calculator. At least 1,000 machines were manufactured. Thomas's invention, named after the inventor and his location as the Thomas deColmar, launched the calculator industry.

Addac, manufactured by the Addac Company, Houseman Building in Grand Rapids, Michigan. This machine was first placed on the market in April of 1926, but by 1928 production was halted. It is a nine column adding and subtracting machine. To add, the operator inserted a finger into a notch at a number and then slid it down until the finger struck the base plate. To subtract, the reverse was done. The Addac's original selling price was $24.50. Dimensions: 5" h x 8" w. Value: $150.

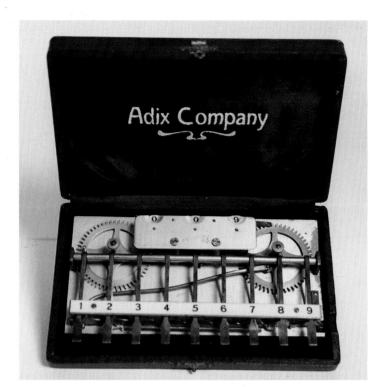

Adix, manufactured by the Adix Company, circa 1909. It is a unique adding machine. With only nine keys and an all exposed mechanism, you are able to see how the mechanical movements work together to provide the end results. Dimensions: 5.5" h x 2.75" w. Value: $800.

Argos II, manufactured by Gesellschaft für Präzionstechnick G.m.b.H., Alte Jakob Strasse 20, Berlin SW 68, Germany. The serial number of the pictured unit is 2,183 and was manufactured in 1913. Dimensions: 2.25" w x 5.25" long. Value: $800.

Arithstyle, manufactured by Gesellschaft für Machinenbau und Elektrishe Neuheiten G. m. b. H., Hafenplaz, 5 Berlin, Germany. The Arithstyle is a hand-held, chain driven, nine column adding machine. The Arithstyle Company holds a 1911 copyright. The machine pictured is serial number 11,698. The first and last patent dates are January 3, 1899 and May 3, 1910. Dimensions: 2.25" w x 5" long. Value: $600-$800.

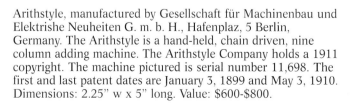

Baldwin Arithmometer, invented by F.S. Baldwin and patented July 28, 1874. This was one of Frank Baldwin's first inventions that pertained to adding machines or calculators. It was called an "Arithmometer or Accountant's Assistant." Dimensions: 5.25" long x 4.75" w. Rare. Value: $9,000.

Britannic, manufactured in England by Guys Calculating Machines, Ltd., Wood Green, London N22, England and distributed by The Muldivo Calculating Machines Co., Ltd., 49 Queen Victoria Street, London, England. The serial number of the pictured unit is 1,932. The Britannic is a very attractive version of the Brunsviga type. Dimensions: 9.5" w x 4" h x 4" d. Scarce. Value: $500.

Brunsviga Midget, manufactured by Grimme, Natalis and Company of Braunschweig, Germany around 1892. It is very popular and considered to be a very collectible pinwheel calculator. The Brunsviga was based on the Original Odhner patents. Value: $300.

Curta No. 1, manufactured by Contina AG Mauren Liechtenstein. The serial number of the pictured machine is 55,726. The Curta resembles a pepper mill more than it does a calculator. Nevertheless, it is considered to be very collectible. Dimensions: 2" diameter x 4" h. Value: $600.

Felt & Tarrant Comptometer, manufactured by Felt & Tarrant Manufacturing Company of Chicago, Illinois. Dorr E. Felt was the inventor and it appeared on the market in 1887. The serial number of the pictured machine is 408. One of Felt's first patents was 366,945 dated July 19, 1887. While not the world's first "key driven calculator," it was the most successfully marketed. Felt's initial invention was made out of a wooden macaroni box and it is still fondly referred to as that. His first manufactured machine was also housed in a wooden box but all the parts were metal. These models all carried serial numbers below 15,000. Dimensions: 7.25" w x 14.25" long. Rare. Value: $2,500–$3,500.

Dalton, manufactured by the Dalton Adding Machine Company of Popular Bluff, Missouri. Hubert Hopkins was the inventor and it was patented on August 1, 1899 under patent number 630,053. The serial number of the pictured machine is 8,422. This is an important machine. It was one of the first 10 key adding machine that also printed. Up to this time, they were either full keyboard machines, or 10 key machines that could not print. A collector is especially interested in the earlier version, or the first model of this adding machine, which had beveled glass on side and front panels. Dimensions: 11.25" h x 9.50" w x 14" d. Value: $300.

Feliks, manufactured by Schetmash in the city of Kursk, Russia around 1935. The serial number of the pictured machine is 28,331. The Feliks is a Russian calculator along the same lines as the popular Brunsviga. Dimensions: 11" w x 5.50" h x 5.50" d. Scarce. Value: $300.00.

Comptograph. In 1888, Felt realized there was a need for a recording or printing calculator. He developed one and was granted patent number 465,255 on December 15, 1891. This is the only model known to exist by the author. Not many were manufactured and, therefore, it is quite rare. (Other calculators developed by Felt and Tarrant are more common and usually can be found under $100.) Dimensions: 17.25" d x 10.25" w x 11.50" h. Value: $8.000+.

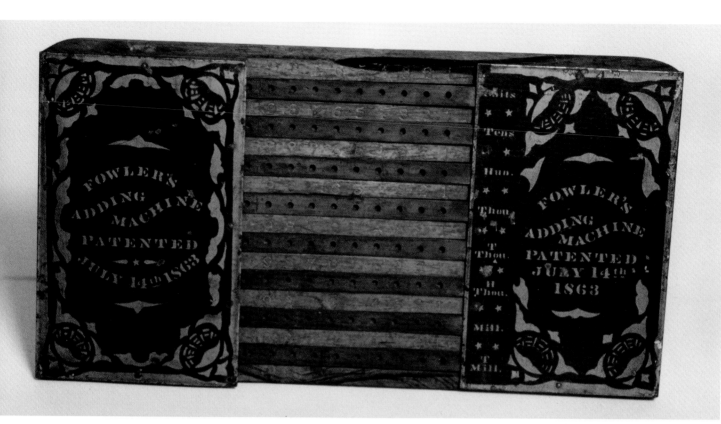

Fowler's Adding Machine, manufactured by the Fowler Adding Machine Company at 212 Broadway at the corner of Fulton Street, New York, New York. It carries July 14, 1863 as its patent date. It is a slide bar type adding machine. Addition is performed on the front of the machine and the results appear in a window on the reverse side of the unit. Dimensions: 4.5" long x 8.75" w. Rare.
Value: $1,000.

Groesbeck's Calculating Machine, manufactured by Ziegler and McCurdy and marketed through S. H. Crittenden & Company at 1131 Chestnut Street, Philadelphia, Pennsylvania. It was patented on March 1, 1870. The specimen pictured has five (5) place settings on both the adding and subtracting registers. Dimensions: 3" h x 6.5" w. Rare. Value: $3,000.

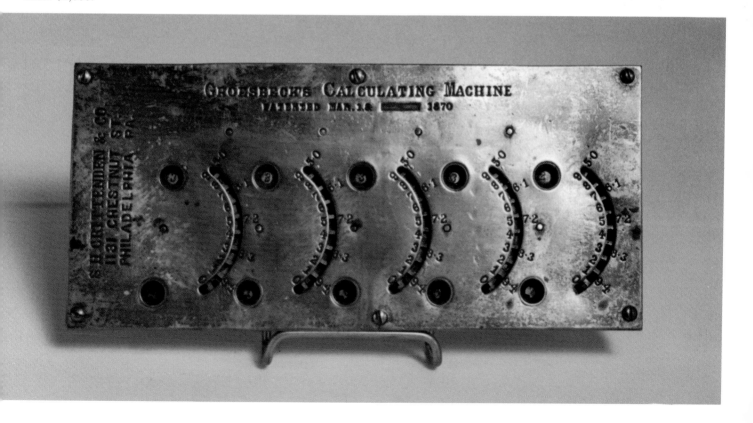

Hart Adding Machine, manufactured by the Scoville Manufacturing Company of Waterbury, Connecticut and distributed by the J. S. Strange Steel Letter Cutter Company of Bangor, Maine. The inventor was William Hart of Kirksville, Missouri and he holds patent number 199,289 dated January 15, 1878. The Hart adder was a paddle-like instrument with four rows of numbers arranged cylindrically. Each row worked independently and could be rotated to line up with a pointer. Dimensions: 8" long, 5" diameter. Rare. Value: $5,000+.

Right:
Hatfield Adder, invented and manufactured by A.L. (Aaron) Hatfield of Lewisburg, Pennsylvania. He holds patent number 11,726 dated September 26, 1854. The unit pictured is serial number 345. It is constructed of walnut and brass. There are three (3) bands of numbers arranged cylindrically and they appear to be hand stamped. The inventor described his instrument as "a series of circular metallic disks, having numbers stamped thereon, so arranged in connection with springs, that by the alternative movement of a lever, any number of figures, from 1 to 10,000 or more may be correctly and easily added together before the eye." Since only a few other examples of the Hatfield adder are known to exist, it is considered to be rare. Dimensions: 9.75" long x 4.75" diameter. Value: $5,500+.

Key Adding Machine, manufactured by J. F. Key of 942 Santee Street, Los Angeles, California. The serial number of the pictured machine is 480. The Key adder used two large circular discs that could be rotated using a stylus. Operating instructions are printed on the bottom of the machine. Dimensions: 13.75" long x 5.50" d x 4.5" h. Rare. Value: $1,000.

Leavitt Interest Calculator, stereotyped by Morill Silsby & Company of New Hampshire and invented by William B. Leavitt by Act of Congress in 1845. A primitive, wood framed disc that is 12.25" in diameter and computes interest from 1.00 to 1,000.00. Dimensions: 12.25" diameter. Scarce. Value: $600.

Lightning, a cardboard adder with 10s carry ability. Instructions are printed on the reverse side as indicated by the second photograph. Inventor and manufacturer are unknown to the author at the present time. Dimensions: 6.75" w x 7.25" h. Rare. Value: $650.

Locke Adder, manufactured by the C. E. Locke Manufacturing Company, Kensett, Iowa. The two patents located on the Locke are December 24, 1901 on the earlier model and January 3, 1905 on the later one. The Locke was a slide bar type with eight (8) bars that could be slid back and forth to add figures together. Dimensions: 10.75" w x 4" h. Scarce. Value: $600.

Above and right:
Marchant. The Marchant Calculator Company began its operation in Oakland, California in 1911. The first models were of the pinwheel variety, but in 1923 a mechanical keyboard was introduced. Prices vary according to the model but the two machines pictured normally sell for $150 each, depending on their condition.

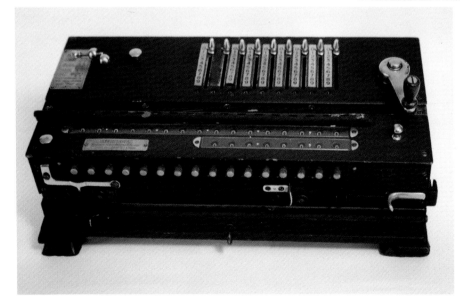

Mercedes-Euklid, manufactured by the Mercedes Office Machine Works of Charlottenburg 2, Berlin Street 153, Germany. Its designer was Christian Hamann, also of Berlin, c. 1905. The Mercedes was a lever-set calculator that boasted automatic division, automatic carriage movement and a one stroke clearing action. Dimensions: 14.5" w x 9" d x 6.25" h. Scarce. Value: $800.

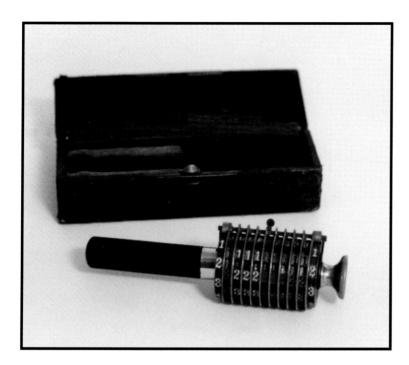

Midget Adding Machine, manufactured by the Midget Sales Company, 60 Van Buren Street, Brooklyn, New York, around 1910. The Midget was a stylus-type, hand-held, adding machine. The operator held the unit by the handle with the left hand. The little finger of the right hand was used to depress the knob at the other end of the device while simultaneously using the remaining fingers of the right hand to add the numbers wanted through the use of a pencil or stylist. A very awkward operation at best. Dimensions: 4" long x 1" diameter. Rare. Value: $5,000.

Millionaire, invented by Otto Steiger St. Gallen in 1893 and manufactured by H.W. Egli, A. G., Zurick, Switzerland. A very heavy four function, lever-type calculator that was considered to be fast for its time, especially in multiplication. Dimensions: 25.5" w x 11" d x 7" h. Scarce. Value: $2,000–$3,000.

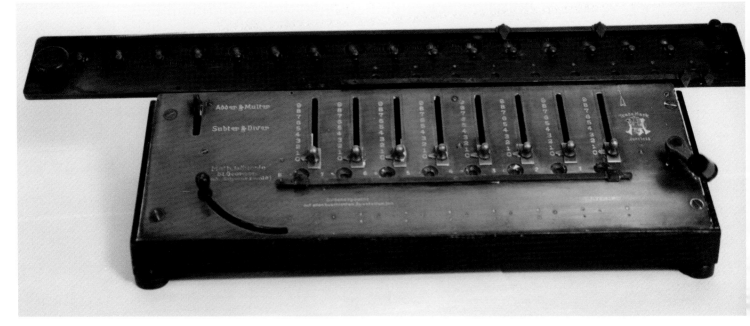

Peerless Arithmometer, manufactured by Math. Bäuerle at St. Georgen in the Black Forest, Germany about 1904. The Peerless was of the stepped drum mechanical principle, first developed by Thomas de Colmar and commonly called an "Arithmometer." The first Peerless was enclosed in a wooden base and then in metal as pictured. Later models used keytops instead of levers as the setting mechanism. Dimensions: 12.5" w x 7.75" d x 4.5" h. Rare. Value: Approximately $2,500.

Quixsum Fractional Adding Machine, manufactured by the Precision Adding Machine Company, Inc. of Providence, Rhode Island and Charlotte, North Carolina. The serial number of the pictured unit is 2,759. It is a Model C and was manufactured in 1924. This adding machine had the ability to add fractions, inches, feet, and hundreds. Dimensions: 6" long x 16.25" w. Scarce. Value: $1,500-$2,000.

Above and right:
Spalding. The inventor of this adding machine was C. G. Spalding and he was granted patents on January 13, 1874 and February 19, 1874. The serial number of the pictured machine is 723. The Spalding had nine keys set below two circular dials. One entered units and the other entered hundreds. The Spalding is said to be one of the first machines to carry tens. The second photograph shows the mechanism it used. Dimensions: 7" h x 7" w. Rare. Value: $8,000-$10,000.

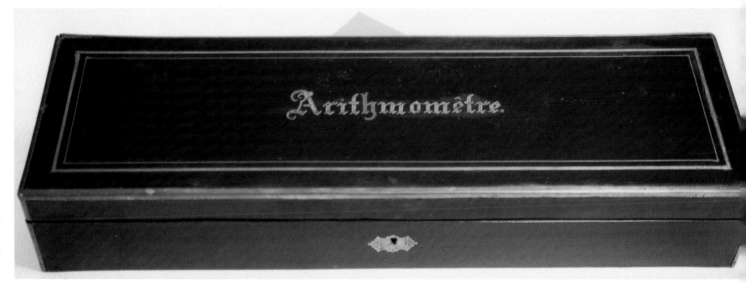

Thomas deColmar Arithmomêtre. Charles Xavier Thomas was the inventor of this calculator. He incorporated the mechanical stepped drum principle, which was used in many other calculators during later years. The Thomas machine was manufactured by the Compagnie d'Assurance le Phénix at 33 rue du Helder, Paris, France. Thomas also acted as manager of this company. This calculator is considered to be the first commercially successful calculator and launched the calculator industry. It was first introduced in 1820 and continued in production for well over 60 years. Dimensions: 23" w x 7" d x 4" h. Serial number: 725. Rare. Value: $10,000-$12,000.

TIM, manufactured around 1907 by Ludwig Spitz and Company of Berlin, Templehof, Eresburgstr. The name of the machine, "TIM" is an acronym for "Time Is Money." Dimensions: 21.5" w x 6" d x 6.75" h. Rare. Value: $500-$750.

Triumph Adding Machine, manufactured by the Triumph Adding Machine Company of Brooklyn, New York. It was patented on February 13, 1907 and May 11, 1908. The serial number of the pictured machine is 1,067. The Triumph's claim to fame was that it only had four working parts. The register was activated by placing one figure on the number desired and pulling a chain all the way down. Dimensions: 9.50" long x 7.50" h x 7" d. Scarce. Value: $1,500-$2,000.

Below and right:
Universal Adding Machine, manufactured by the Universal Adding Machine Company, 358 Pearl Street, New York, New York. It was patented on July 15, 1890. Another slide bar stylus-type adding machine, it originally had a suggested retail price of $8. Dimensions: 9.25" long x 4.25" h. Rare. Value: $1,000 approximately.

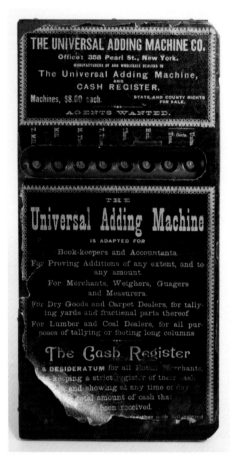

Webb (The Adder), patented by C.H. Webb on November 5, 1889. This stylus-type adder is often referred to as the "Figure Eight Machine" for obvious reasons. This particular model is in a wooden carrying case and also houses the original stylus. Dimensions: 4.25" w x 6.25" h. Scarce. Value: $600 (with case).

# CHAPTER II

# ADVERTISING, PICTURES, POST CARDS, AND INK BLOTTERS

## ADVERTISING:

To the collector of office technologies, advertising is more than just an attractive way to decorate your displayed collection. It is an excellent source of information for the office antique historian.

Many office equipment manufacturers announced new products through the advertising media. Those announcements not only told the public the introduction date of a particular product, but included a description of new features that were engineered into that model.

Some advertisements showed the date when manufacturing first began; information about the inventor; and an anniversary announcement in addition to information about any current models and/or enhancements.

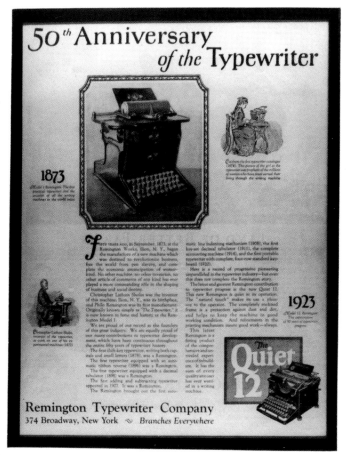

Remington 50th Anniversary advertisement for their typewriter is a good example of the practice of introducing new products.

Dictaphone Dictating Machine advertisement in the *Saturday Evening Post* of October 23, 1920. Value: $6.

IBM Electromatic Typewriter
advertisement. (c. 1932) Value: $6.

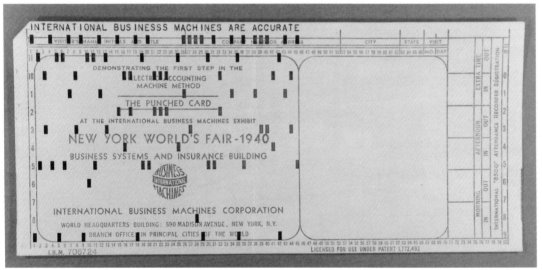

Above and right:
An actual IBM punch
card distributed at the
1940 World's Fair in
New York to advertise
the IBM Accounting
System. Value: $40.

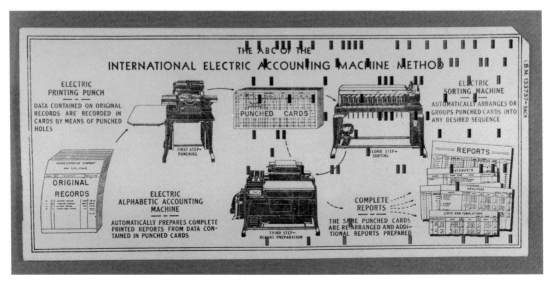

Four (4) copier manufacturer advertisements: Haloid Xerox,
*Fortune Magazine*, 1959; ThermoFax, *Fortune Magazine* (c.
1950); Transcopy, *Fortune Magazine*, 1958; Speed-0-Print
*Fortune Magazine*, 1959. Value: $6-$10 each.

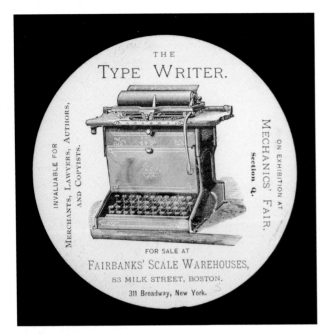

Sholes & Glidden Typewriter as advertised by Fairbanks Scale Company, New York, New York. (c. 1878) 2" diameter: Value: $50.

Right and below:
Advertising brochure for the Hooven Automatic Typewriter. Value: $50.

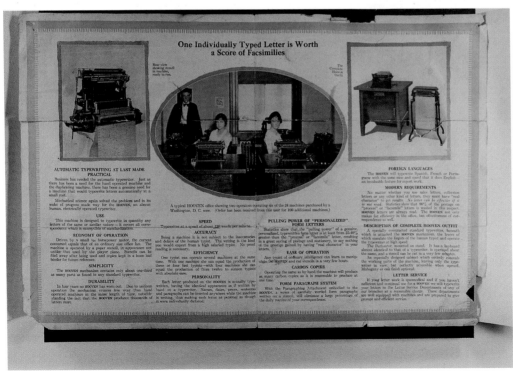

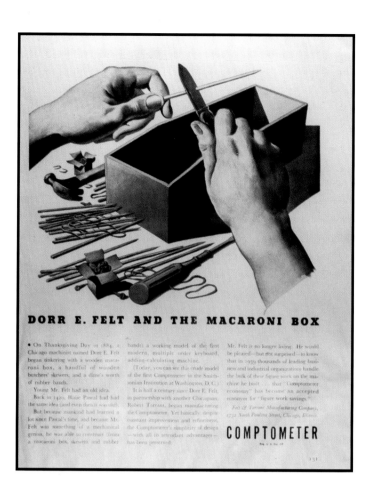

Felt and Tarrant Comptometer Company historical information advertisement extolling the time, method and concept of the prototype Comptometer of 1884. Value: $15.

McCaskey cash register in the *Saturday Evening Post* of March 21, 1927. Value: $6.

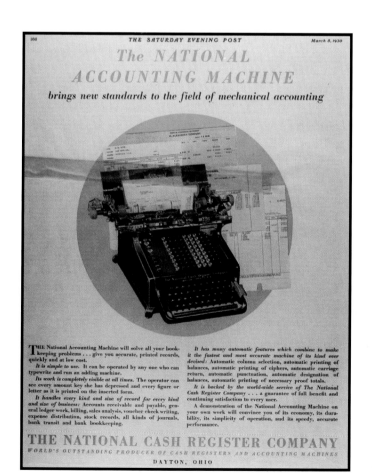

NCR (National Cash Register) Accounting Machine advertisement from the *Saturday Evening Post* of March 8, 1930. Value: $6.

An advertisement announcing a Remington Typewriter capable of adding and subtracting. Value: $6.

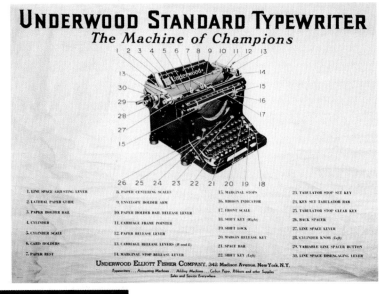

Above and left:
Advertising in the form of two classroom teaching aids. One is a keyboard diagram of a Remington. The other identifies the parts of an Underwood typewriter. Value: $50 each.

This page:
Three typewriter advertisements: Remington (*Saturday Evening Post* of November 29, 1914); Royal (*Saturday Evening Post* of January 19, 1929); and, Underwood (*Saturday Evening Post* of 1922). Value Each: $6.

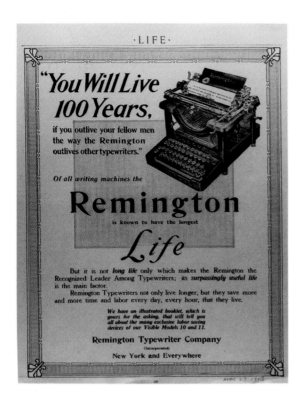

Remington Quiet Deluxe KMC
Typewriter 1948 announcement in
*Fortune Magazine.*

Remington advertisement in *Life Magazine*
concerning the longevity and durability of their
product. (c.1947) Value $6.

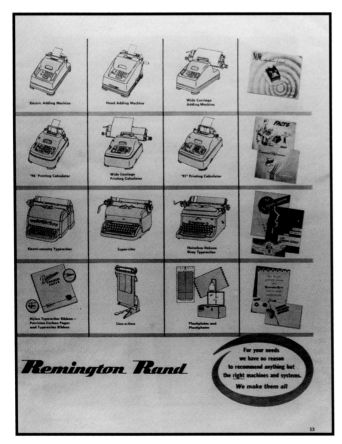

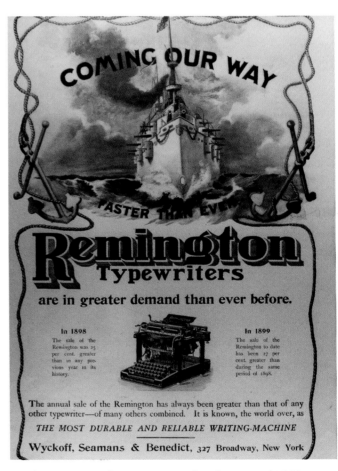

Remington Typewriter Company advertisement of 1899
boasting of a twenty-five percent (25%) or better increase in
sales for two (2) consecutive years. Value: $15.

Remington Rand advertisement of their entire office product
line. (c. 1950) Value: $4.

Remington Typewriter Company targets the children's market with this Mickey Mouse advertisement. (c.1930) Value: $4.

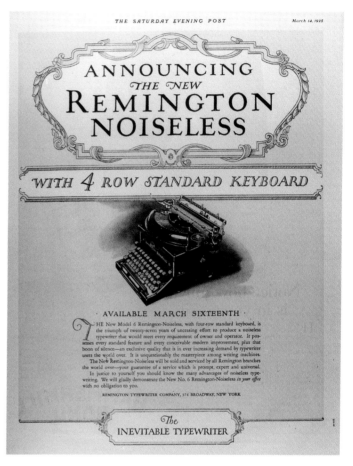

Announcement advertisement in the *Saturday Evening Post* of May 14, 1925. Remington Noiseless Typewriter Company advertisement announcing they were changing from a 3-row keyboard (Model 5) to a 4-row keyboard (Model 6). Value: $15.

Left:
75th Year Anniversary advertisement by Remington that appeared in the *Saturday Evening Post* in 1948. Value $15.

This advertisement appeared in the *Saturday Evening Post* in 1923. It also announced that Remington was the first manufacturer to introduce the following features: Automatic Ribbon Reverse; Decimal Tabulation; first combination Adding and Subtracting Typewriter; and the first line indenting mechanism. In many of the pictures and advertisements, ladies were encouraged to pose with the equipment. These early women models gave us a glimpse of the office fashions and hairstyles of the period. Value: $10.

The L.C. Smith & Corona Typewriter Company announced their "Animal Keyboard" machine targeting the children's market. A set of nine rings were provided by the manufacturer to help children learn how to type. A ring was worn on each finger and one thumb. They matched the animals on the keytops and was intended to encourage children to use the proper finger to strike each key. Value: $20.

Underwood Bookkeeping Machine in the *Literary Digest* of December 28, 1918. Value: $6.

Left, below left and above:
Three Underwood advertisements from the *Saturday Evening Post*: The Underwood Elliott Fisher of 1936; Underwood Electric of 1947; and, Underwood Portable of 1950. Value each: $4.

Victor Adding Machine banner. (c. 1950) Value $25.

# PICTURES

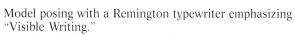
Model posing with a Remington typewriter emphasizing "Visible Writing."

Above right, right, and below:
Pictures of the Automatic Bookkeeping cash registers and their home office in Kansas City, Missouri. (c. 1915) Each valued at $200.

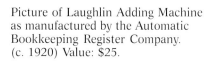

Picture of banner awarded to the Automatic Bookkeeping Register Company for the Gold Medal at the 1915 Pan American Exposition. Value: $25.

Picture of Laughlin Adding Machine as manufactured by the Automatic Bookkeeping Register Company. (c. 1920) Value: $25.

Early picture of the Densmore Typewriter shown from three different positions with a female model of that period. Value: $350.

## FIFTY FAMOUS FINGERS
### NOW WRITE WITH
## REMINGTON NOISELESS PORTABLE TYPEWRITERS

THE Guardians of the Dionne Quintuplets, the world's most scientifically reared children, recently decided to give their five little charges the advantages of typewriters in their education. The Remington Noiseless Portable was the writing machine they chose. ¶Remington Rand, proud of this selection, combined the resources of professional educators, crack engineers, skilled technicians—produced a new, exclusive, 5-purpose *Educational Keyboard* . . . promptly named it in honor of the Quintuplets. ¶This keyboard is standard in every respect and will write eight languages—and simple mathematics. It can be used for work in kindergarten, elementary grades, high school and college in addition to the many uses for home and business writing. *It will prepare children to use any standard typewriter in the future.* ¶Emilie, Cecile, Marie, Annette and Yvonne (as they appear from left to right on the oil painting made especially for this reproduction) were able to write their full names shortly after receiving their Remington Noiseless Typewriters. They have even typed letters to their beloved Dr. Dafoe, as well as their charming Queen Elizabeth of England.

"Fifty Famous Fingers" picture of the Dionne Quintuplets with five Remington Noiseless Portable Typewriters. In honor of the birth of the quintuplets, the Remington Typewriter Company designed a new exclusive five purpose educational keyboard and appropriately named it the Dionne keyboard. This is a picture of a print of the painting by Alex Levy in 1940. Each typewriter has the name of one of the girls on it, i.e. Emilie, Cecile, Marie, Annette and Yvonne.

These were classroom-teaching aids distributed by Remington. Miss Remington says: "You must learn before you can earn." Dimensions: 11.5" x 21.5". Value: $125.

Miss Remington says: "Accuracy First." Dimensions: 11.5" x 21.5". Value: $125.

Miss Remington says: "Use the Column Selector." Dimensions: 11.5" x 21.5". Value: $125.

A poster sold by the Business Technology Association (BTA). Originally created in 1989 to honor the inventor of the typewriter and the QWERTY keyboard. The typewriter in the picture is one of the first Sholes & Glidden typewriters that were introduced on a sewing machine stand. The typewriter pictured in the poster is in the collection of the Clark family of Connecticut. Poster value: $25.

Remington Model 7 with a female secretary. Picture caption reads "Comrades." Copyrighted 1903 by Remington Rand. Value: $300.

Remington Typewriter Model 6 with a secretary, marked "Central Bureau of Engineering, New York." Value: $600.

In 1920, the Remington Typewriter Company distributed a large picture of Christopher Latham Sholes, the inventor of America's first successful typewriter, to typing classes throughout the country. A long line of women were superimposed in the background stretching off into the distance. A quote from the inventor was printed below which stated "I feel that I have done something for the women, who have always had to work so hard. This will enable them more easily to earn a living." Value: $500.

**Remington Rand Manufacturing Plants**

Remington Noiseless, Standard and Portable Typewriters . . Remington, Powers and Dalton Accounting Machines
Kardex, Library Bureau, Baker Vawter· Kalamazoo Systems Equipment . . The Safe-Cabinet

A collage of Remington Rand
manufacturing plants which included
Remington Typewriters; Remington
Noiseless Typewriters; Kardex (Systems);
Dalton Adding Machines; Baker Vawter;
Library Bureau and Powers Tabulating. All
were companies James Rand later
consolidated into one: the Remington
Rand Company. Value: $250.

Left and above:
Two large pictures of the new electric and manual
Royal Typewriters with female models. Dimensions:
39" w x 33" h. Value: $300 each.

Telephone Switchboard
Operator. (c. 1940)
Value: $75.

Rendering of an Underwood Typewriter marked
"Red Writer." A lithograph from an original silk
screen print by Anne Duncan of Alexandria,
Virginia. Value: $20.

Williams Typewriter Company tin sign. Value: $300.

## POST CARDS

Postcards have preserved much of the office culture of the early 1900s. There were post cards that revealed the office humor of the day and some that boasted about the office product, but my favorites were those that pictured our great manufacturing facilities of the period.

Angel and typewriter post card dated 1906. Value: $4.

Baby with Typewriter post card, "Drop Me A Line." Value: $3.

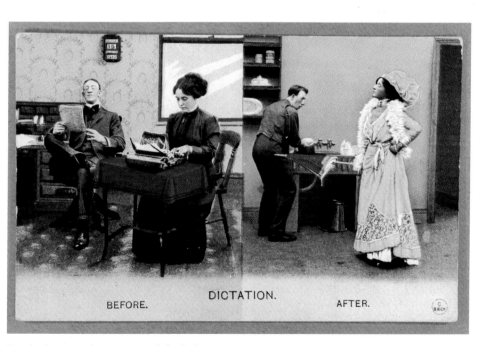

Bar lock typewriter post card depicting an attempt at "office humor," dated 1913. Value: $14.

Post card showing a child
with an unidentified
typewriter. (c.1914)
Value: $6.

Dainty demure she sits & works

Commercial Visible
Typewriter post card.
Value: $3.50.

CORONA TYPEWRITER CO., Groton, N. Y.

Corona Typewriter Factory,
Groton, New York.
Value: $6.

Three Easter chicks in office. (c.1913) Value: $3.

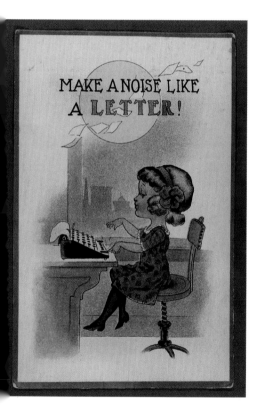

"Make a Noise Like a Letter" post card.
(c.1913) Value: $5.

Monarch Typewriter Factory of
Syracuse, New York. Value: $8.

PLANT OF THE NATIONAL CASH REGISTER CO., DAYTON, O.

National Cash Register Company at Dayton, Ohio. (c.1901) Value: $15.

THE NATIONAL CASH REGISTER CO., DAYTON, OHIO

National Cash Register Company of Dayton, Ohio (c.1950) Value: $8.

Right and far right: Office related post cards called "You're A.1. With Me"and "Rapid Work." Value: $7 each.

YOU'RE A.1.

Office humor post card entitled "Business Demanding Close Attention." (c.1909) Value: $5.

Office humor post card entitled "What Every Woman Knows." Value: $6.

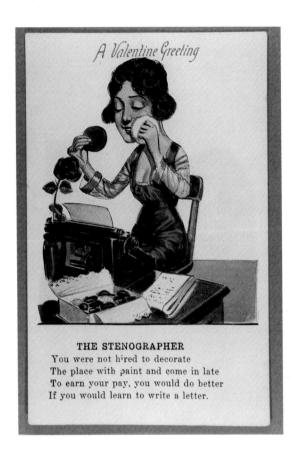

A Valentine Greeting

**THE STENOGRAPHER**
You were not hired to decorate
The place with paint and come in late
To earn your pay, you would do better
If you would learn to write a letter.

Office Valentine post card entitled "The Stenographer." Value: $5.

WOODSTOCK, ILLINOIS

*Plant of* **The OLIVER Typewriter Co.**

Oliver Typewriter "New" plant at Woodstock, Illinois. Value: $10.

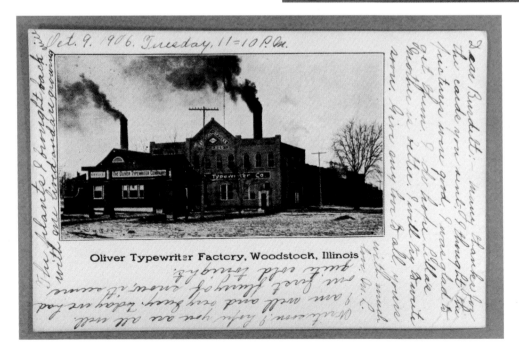

Oliver Typewriter Factory, Woodstock, Illinois

Oliver Typewriter "Old" plant in Woodstock, Illinois. (c.1906) Value: $25.

54

Oliver Typewriter office humor. Value: $10.

Remington Typewriter and Dictation Machine post card. (c.1950) Value: $3.

Remington Typewriter plant in Ilion, New York, dated May 9, 1908. Value: $8.

Remington Typewriter plant of Ilion, New York, dated 1909. Title reads "A few of the skilled employees of Remington Standard Typewriter Factory." Value: $15.

Royal Typewriter plant in Hartford, Connecticut. Value: $10.

L.C. Smith Typewriter factory post card. Value: $8.

Smith Premier Typewriter factory at Syracuse, New York. Value: $5.

"The Typewriter Girl" post card. (c. 1909) Value: $10.

THE TYPEWRITER GIRL
Oh, the belle of the office is she;
Office boy, clerks and boss all agree
That her manners are grand
They are "hers to command!"
Oh, who'd not a typewriter be?

A SECTION OF THE TYPING DEPARTMENT, GOLDEY COLLEGE, WILMINGTON, DELAWARE

Typing class of Goldey College in Wilmington, Delaware post card. (c. 1930) Value: $3.

Right and below:
Underwood Giant Typewriter post cards of the Model 5 as displayed (right) at the Palace of Liberal Arts, Panama-Pacific Exhibition, San Francisco, 1915, and (below) at the Boardwalk Auditorium in Atlantic City, New Jersey. (c. 1935) It was advertised to take three years to build at a cost of $100,000, and weighed 14 tons. Each type bar weighed 45 pounds and the carriage alone weighed 3,500 pounds. Value: $25.

Underwood Master Model post card of machine displayed at the 1939 New York World's Fair. It is believed to be the same internal machine as the Atlantic City Model No. 5 but was retrofitted to look like the Underwood Master.

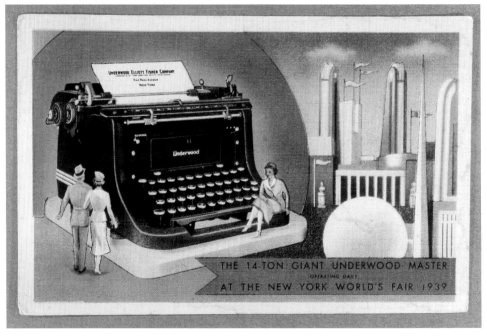

58

Underwood Typewriter Post Card.
Value: $6.

## INK BLOTTERS

Ink blotter,
Burroughs product
line. (c. 1914)
Value: $8.

Ink blotter, Dalton
Adding Machine.
Value: $10.

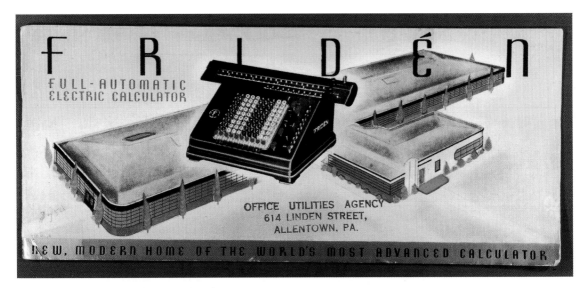

Ink blotter, Friden Calculator. Value: $3.

Ink blotter, Monroe Adding Machine. Value: $3.

Ink blotter, Monroe Adding Machine Model 408-11-092. Value: $5.

Ink blotter, Monroe Bookkeeping Machine. Value: $3.

Ink blotter, National Cash Register "Ask Merchants Service." Value: $3.

Ink blotter, National Adding Machine. Value: $4.

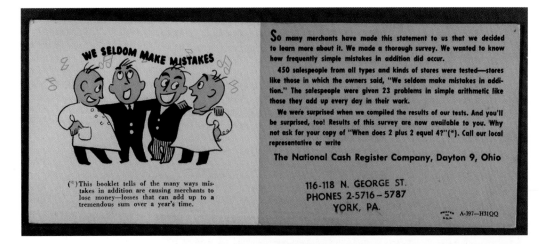

Ink blotter, National Cash Register, "We Seldom Make Mistakes." Value: $6.

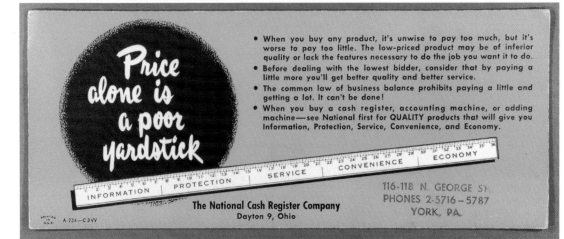

Ink blotter, National Cash Register entitled "Price Alone is a Poor Yardstick." Value: $2.50.

Ink blotter, Wyckoff, Seamans & Benedict, Remington Typewriter No. 6. Value: $10.

Ink blotter, Sundstrand Adding Machine. Value: $3.

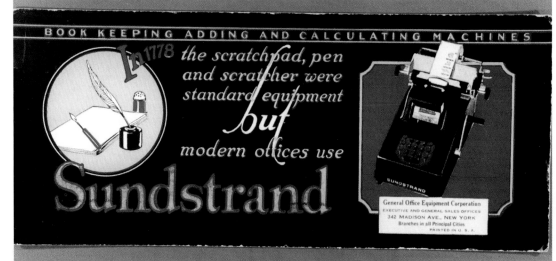

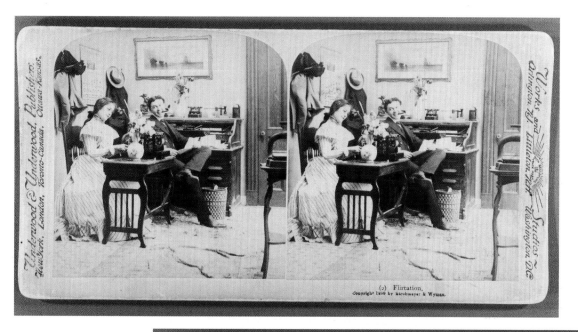

Stereotype picture entitled "Flirtation." Underwood and Underwood Publishers of Washington, D. C. Value: $4.

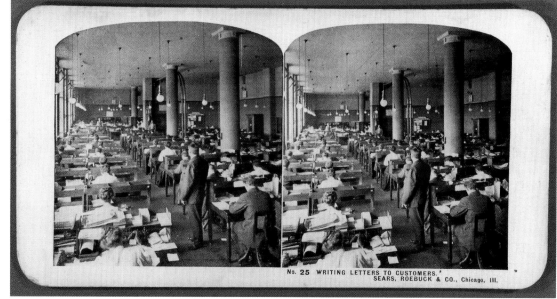

Stereotype picture entitled "Writing Letters to Customers." Sears, Roebuck & Company of Chicago, Illinois. Value: $10.

Ink Blotter, Monroe Calculator. Value: $6.

# CHAPTER III
# CASH REGISTERS, COMBINATION REGISTERS, AUTOGRAPHIC REGISTERS AND COIN CHANGERS

## CASH REGISTERS

The first American cash register was invented by James Ritty in 1878. His company was sold twice and renamed the National Cash Register Company when James Patterson invested in the company in 1883. Patterson eventually took control of the company and began a long and successful domination of the cash register market.

Although cash registers are usually found in retail store environments, they were also used in offices for recording cash, charges, received-on-account and paid-out transactions. At the same time they provided an organized and sequential paper audit trail for each transaction.

The Patterson and NCR story has been told and retold. There were many other cash register manufacturers who attempted to compete in the marketplace. The collection that follows illustrates a sampling of these wonderful machines.

Audit No. 7, one of the many cash registers manufactured by the Michigan Cash Register Company of Detroit, Michigan. (c.1915). Value: $300.

American Cash Register, manufactured by the American Cash Register Company of Saginaw, Michigan. Patent date: July 22, 1911. Formerly the Hallwood Cash Register Company whose roots go back to 1892. Value: $450.

The Automatic Bookkeeping Register was a unique cash register because it truly was three machines in one. First, it was a cash register and, as such, it registered all sales, added and provided totals of cash, credit, and paid out and received on account monies. Second, it was a credit register by accommodating sales slips in separate locked compartments. Third, it performed as an adding machine by providing five separate totals with every transaction printed out on a detail slip. The operator could show the amount of the transaction, the clerk's initials and a description of the transaction. It was a remarkable machine for its day in every way but one. It weighed over 300 pounds. So, it was definitely not portable and was difficult to carry into a retail establishment to demonstrate. It was so huge it took up a great deal of counter space.

The following U. S. patents were granted for what was to become the final Automatic Bookkeeping Register product.

| Patent Number | Date Granted | Application Number | Patentee | Nature Of Owner | Patent |
|---|---|---|---|---|---|
| 13,624 | Mar. 3, 1908 | Re-issue | C.F.Fogg | A.B.R.Co. | Account Register |
| 1,114,085 | Oct. 20, 1914 | 567,128 | G.White | A.B.R.Co. | Register |
| 1,195,309 | Aug.22, 1916 | 805,159 | G.White | A.B.R.Co. | Filing Cabinet |
| 271,466 | July 2,1918 | 21,547 | B.P.Hayes | A.B.R.Co. | Selecting Bar |
| 1,285,156 | Nov. 19, 1918 | 65,334 | B.P.Hayes F.D.Laughlin | A.B.R.Co | Adding Machine |
| 1,340,827 | May 18, 1920 | 113,656 | B.P.Hayes F.D.Laughlin | A.B.R.Co. | Bookkeeping Register |
| 1,362,791 | Dec. 21, 1920 | 373,811 | B.P.Hayes F.D.Laughlin | A.B.R.Co. | Printing Table |
| 1,362.792 | Dec. 21, 1920 | 375,745 | B.P.Hayes F.D.Laughlin | A.B.R.Co. | Printing Table |

Frank Laughlin, Automatic Bookkeeping Register Company President, introduced an all-brass cash register at the 1915 Pan American Exposition, where it won the Gold Medal. The following exhibits are in the author's possession and are a testimonial to their success at the Pan American Exposition.

Exhibit One: Automatic Bookkeeping Register Company all-brass model, serial number 2. Value: $5,000+.

Exhibit Two: Automatic Bookkeeping Register Company Gold Medal.

From these successes, a new production model was developed and venture capital was solicited by going public and selling stock.

Production model used to solicit venture capital with serial number 15. Value: $400-$600.

Exhibit Three: American Bookkeeping Register Company "copy" of Banner.

The Automatic Bookkeeping Register was a great idea for a particular market niche. It sold for $410 and manufacturing costs and boxing the unit to ship, were only $135. But it was not a successful product. Part of the problem may have been its size and weight. It had 6,728 parts and weighed 291.5 pounds exclusive of the shipping box, which weighed an additional 40 to 50 pounds. After producing 1,000 to 1,500 machines, the company went into receivership and eventually closed its doors.

Detroit, manufactured by the Detroit Cash Register Company, Detroit, Michigan and introduced in 1895. The Detroit Cash Register Company was an offshoot of the earlier Seymore Cash Register Company. Value: $500.

Cashier, manufactured by the Cashier Cash Register Company at 1138-46 South Main Street, Los Angeles, California. It was used to weigh gold in California during the gold rush period. Value: $2,000.

Certigraph, manufactured by the Jacksonville Register Company of Jacksonville, Illinois. The Certigraph printed the amount, date and clerk's number on a sales slip that was inserted in the machine. A permanent copy was recorded in a locked compartment within the machine. The Certigraph was designed to prevent negligent or dishonest handling of cash. (c.1920) Value: $300.

Eagle. It is believed that the manufacturer of this cash register was from Milford, Connecticut; however, little is known regarding this very rare cash register at this time. The Eagle is a wooden dial-type cash register. Value: $3,000+.

Dial, manufactured by the Dial Cash Register Company of Milwaukee, Wisconsin. This register resembled the front end of a locomotive more than a cash register. Because of its unique design it is very desirable to a collector. There are not too many around. (c.1915) Value: $8,000-$10,000.

Hallwood Leader, manufactured by the Hallwood Cash Register Company, Columbus, Ohio and introduced around 1892. Value: $400.

Lamson Cash Carrier, manufactured by the Lamson Cash Carrier Company. This was the original Lamson company, which manufactured an overhead conveyor device to carry cash from the cashier to the accounting office. The money was inserted into a capsule suspended from a wire which was used to move it to the accounting office. Value: $150.

Lamson No. 2, manufactured by the Lamson Consolidated Store Service Company of New Jersey and first introduced in 1889. The Lamson is very desirable to collectors. Rare. Value: $3,000+.

Manton Cash and Sales Register invented by Joseph P. Manton, Jr. of Providence, Rhode Island. Patent Number: 449,163 dated March 31, 1891. Value: $350.

Michigan No. 2, manufactured by the Michigan Cash Register Company, Detroit, Michigan and first introduced in 1907. Value: $200.

Monitor, also known as the barber shop register. It consisted of a cash drawer equipped with color coded chips inserted at the top of the unit and normally stored on hangers until the end of the day. At that time, a total could be taken by color and number of chips to be verified against the amount of cash in the drawer. It is usually found without the four containers of color-coded chips mentioned above. Scarce. Value: $500-$700.

National Model 3, manufactured by the National Cash Register Company, Dayton, Ohio. These beautiful custom-designed cases were made of walnut with attractive carvings. They are very collectible. This particular one is serial number 10,822. Value: $2,500-$3,000.

National Total, Adding Cash Register Model 35, manufactured by the National Cash Register Company, Dayton, Ohio. This register also had a clock on the side of the unit to record a clerk's start and stop time. The model pictured above is serial number 82,110. Rare. Value: $2,500-$3,000.

National Cash Register, Model 52, manufactured by the National Cash Register Company, Dayton, Ohio and patented on June 15, 1897. The model above is serial number 329,791. This model was all brass, both the register and the drawer. Value: $800.

Remington Model A-132, manufactured by the Remington Cash Register Company, Inc., a division of the Remington Arms Company of Ilion, New York. (c.1920 / c.1930) Value: $150.

Osborn Imperial, manufactured by the Osborn Cash Register Company, Ltd., Detroit, Michigan. The front cover could be raised to expose the cash drawer. (c.1891) Value: $2,000.

Security, manufactured by the Hough Cash Register Company, Springfield, Massachusetts. Value: $400.

St. Louis, manufactured by the St. Louis Cash Register Company, St. Louis, Missouri. An index-type cash register, it allowed the operator to select the amount of the sale by moving an indicator to the desired number. Many were sold because of its low retail price. (c.1911- c.1920) Value: $300.

Union, manufactured by the Union Cash Register Company, Trenton, New Jersey. (c.1889) The Union was one of the many inventions of one of the greatest cash register inventors of the 20th century, F.L. Fuller. Value: $1,000.

Sun No. 10, manufactured by the Sun Manufacturing Company, Greenfield, Ohio. (c.1891) An interesting and unique system using tiny marbles or steel balls which dropped into the register at the time of sale. On demand the operator could lift the lid and see how much of each denomination had been received. It also had a two-row keyboard if the owner preferred not to use the marbles or steel balls. Value: $1,500.

United States (US), manufactured by the United States Cash Register Company, Detroit, Michigan. (c.1893) Value: $1,000.

Waddel, manufactured by the Waddel Wooden Ware Works Company, Greenfield, Ohio. (c.1891) The Waddel was a wooden register. At the conclusion of a sale the operator inserted a marble in the hole that matched the amount of the sale. At any given time, the owner could unlock the cover and determine the number of nickels, dimes, etc. that had been collected up to that time. It was a simple method that required little mechanical ingenuity or parts. Value: $2,000.

## COMBINATION REGISTERS

During the 1920s a new concept of putting an adding machine on a cash drawer was developed. The idea was to be able to use the cash register as an adding machine. The total key would usually open the cash drawer automatically.

In addition to being inexpensive, the combination register offered the advantage of providing the customer with a printed tape of the transaction. It gave the small grocery store owners what they needed at less cost than the elaborate brass cash registers. It is no wonder that so many were sold and are still found at antique marketplaces today.

Add-Index, a combination of an Add-Index adding machine and a cash drawer manufactured by the Add-Index Corporation, Grand Rapids, Michigan. (c.1925) Value: $200.

American, manufactured by the American Adding Machine Company, Chicago, Illinois around 1920. It was a marriage between the American No. 5 adding machine and a cash drawer. Value: $150.

National Model 202 Desk Autographic Register, manufactured by the National Cash Register Company, Dayton, Ohio. (c.1902) It was a combination oak drawer and desk with a roll of paper on which the sale was recorded. Value: $275.

Dalton, manufactured by the Dalton Adding Machine Company, Cincinnati, Ohio. (c.1920) The Dalton was referred to as an "adding machine combination register." This essentially was a Dalton adding machine mounted on a wooden cash drawer. Value: $175.

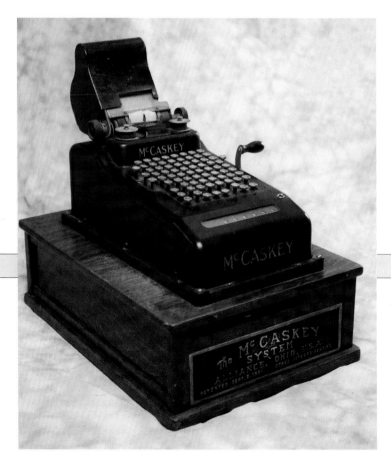

McCaskey, manufactured by the McCaskey Register Company, Alliance, Ohio. An adding machine combined with an inexpensive cash drawer. As a result, thousands were sold and are still to be found in abundance. Value: $175-$300.

National Credit File Model 100, manufactured by the National Cash Register Company of Dayton, Ohio. An easy system of storing and retrieving credit sales slips. Value: $300.

Underwood Sundstrand, manufactured by the Underwood Sundstrand Company. A combination of a Sundstrand adding machine and a cash drawer, available in a variety of models in which the adding machine portion could be equipped with either of two carriage sizes with a 6 or 7 column capacity. (c.1920) Value: $150.

## AUTOGRAPHIC REGISTERS

The Standard, manufactured by the Standard Autographic Register Company, Dayton, Ohio. Model S-5. Value: $50.

Pioneer Model B-1, manufactured by the Shoup Autographic Register Company, Hamilton, Ohio. Patent Date: October 9, 1882. Rare. Value: $250.

## COIN CHANGERS

You may think of a coin changer as part of a retail or bank environment rather than an office device. However, they were used in many corporate payroll departments of factories and larger businesses.

The two most common types of coin changers were the "payer" type and the "changer" type. The payer type would deliver the amount according to the key depressed. For instance if you depressed the key marked 25, the machine would deliver $.25 in change.

The changer type was designed to deliver the difference between the sale amount and the amount tendered. For example if you received $1.00 on the purchase of a $.25 item and you depressed the key marked $.25, the machine would deliver $.75 change.

Autocash Model V, USA, manufactured by the American AutoCash Corporation, New York. The pictured unit's serial number is 1,146. A five (5) coin model with two shuttles for nickels and dimes. Finished in mahogany grain paint on metal, this was a payer type unit. Dimensions: 13" h x 11.5" w x 6" d. Value: $125.

Brandt Model K, manufactured by the Brandt Cashier Company, Watertown, Wisconsin. The pictured machine is serial number of 20,254. The patent dates listed are: July 9, 1895; May 24, 1898; October 2, 1900; July 3, 1906; March 10, 1896; July 11, 1899; June 24, 1902; May 25, 1909 and October 15, 1912. Dimensions: 9" h x 8.25" w x 8" d. Brandt manufactured both the payer and changer types. The specimen shown is a changer type. Value: $350.

Brandt, brass earlier version, manufactured by the Brandt Cashier Company, Watertown, Wisconsin. A solid brass unit elaborately engraved with the initial B on both sides. Value: $400.

Lightning, manufactured by the Lightning Coin Changer Company, Chicago, Illinois. The pictured unit's serial number is 13,567 and patent dates of November 27 and September 4, 1917. It was a payer type with 26 keys that were color-coded. Later models were available as either payer or changer types. Dimensions: 12" h x 11" w x 12" d. Value: $150.

Potter Model 17, manufactured by the Coin Machine Manufacturing Company, Portland, Oregon. The unit pictured has a serial number of 1,647 and notes that patents were applied for. It was nickel-plated with three banks of key tops. The top row has the numerals $5, $4, $2, $1 (reading from left to right). The second row (reading from left to right) has key tops as follows: a 1912 half dollar; a 1911 Quarter; two 1910 dimes and a 1912 nickel. The third row has seven key tops. All were Indian Head pennies (1902, 1903, 1898, 1899, 1895, 1903, and 1897). Dimensions: 13" h x 11.75" w x 11.5" d. Value: $350.

Universal. Although called a cash register, the Universal was really a coin changer. It was made to fit a regular cash drawer so change could be made easily. It was patented in 1894. Value: $25.

# CHAPTER IV
# CHECK PROTECTORS

A skilled and unethical individual can alter a check in a number of ways. Common alterations would include changes to the name of the payee, the amount of the check, or the signature of the creator of the transaction. Banks are obligated to honor forged signatures, but any other alteration became the responsibility of the payee.

Most companies began to pay their accounts payable invoices and their employee payrolls with checks. So a market developed for a device that would supply these companies with a measure of security. The devices created for this need were the check protector, check punch, check perforator, and the check writer. They proved efficient enough to protect the date, payee's name, and the dollar amount of the check. The amount of the check was printed numerically as well as spelled out alphabetically.

Machines began appearing around the 1870s, and by the 1920s there were at least 20 manufacturers participating in this segment of the office technology market.

The collecting of check writers has become an increasingly popular past time in the last several years. Machines can be found at flea markets as well as in antique malls. This popularity makes them a good investment for the future as their value continues to increase.

Abbott Check Protector. The Abbott was invented by Edwin O. Abbott of Chicago, Illinois and patented on April 23, 1889. The Abbott has a cast iron base upon which a shell-like casing surrounds the major parts of the machine. A dial plate upon which the numerals 1, 2, 3, 4, 5, 6, 7, 8, 9 and 0 are engraved encloses the top of the casing. The symbols include a dollar sign ($) and an asterisk (*). There are two levers of different sizes on top of the machine. The smaller lever has a little knob at its free end. This lever is connected to a center post and when the knob is lifted by one hand, the other hand turns the dial face to the numeral and/or symbol desired. Once this proper character is selected, the operator depresses the larger lever to punch that character or symbol on the check in a pattern of small holes. This technique is repeated until the entire amount of the check is finally punched out. Of course this technique required a steady hand and eye or the printed amount would waver slightly. The manufacturer was the Abbott Check Perforator Company of Chicago, Illinois and the machine pictured has a serial number of 895. Dimensions: 6" h x 7.25" w x 7" d. Scarce. Value: $150-$200.

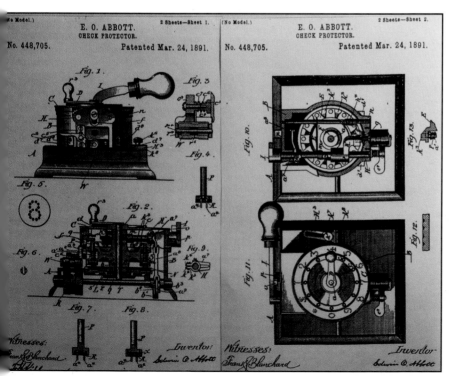

American Perforator, manufactured by American Perforator Company at 624 W. Jackson Boulevard of Chicago, Illinois. It perforated characters and numerals in a dot like pattern. Small removable levers resembling cribbage pegs are used to reset the desired numbers to be punched. Dimensions: 6" h x 7.25" w x 10" d. Common. Value: $75.

Arnold Check Writer. The Arnold was a hand held portable check protector. The operator held the unit in their right hand and depressed the feed release with the right thumb. With their left hand they fed the paper through the mechanism. A knob located on the left side of the unit turned the wheel to the desired numeral. Then the operator punched the numeral onto the paper by squeezing the handle with the right hand. The paper check is automatically advanced to the next position and the procedure needs to be done again until the entire amount is perforated. It was manufactured by Arnold, Incorporated, of Flint, Michigan, and its patent number is 1,201,235. (c.1917) Common. Value: $125-$175.

Beebe Indelible Check Protector (A). There were at least two models of the Beebe Indelible. The earlier model had three patent dates, February 11, 1896; February 16, 1897 and November 23, 1897. This model was red and decorated with gold stenciling. The top of the unit and the front plate were nickel-plated. Common. Value: $125.

Beebe indelible Check Protector (B). The second model was manufactured in Rochester, New York and had six patent dates, February 11, 1896; February 11, 1896 (Canadian); February 11, 1896 (Great Britain); February 16, 1897; March 21, 1905, and September 26, 1905. Common. Value: $125.

Their second model is nickel plated and had a more modern release lever on the left side. It also shows the manufacturer as the B. F. Cummins Company, Chicago, Illinois and New York, New York. Scarce. Value: $125-$225.

Chicago Check Perforator, manufactured by the Chicago Check Protector Company, Bonn Brothers in New York, New York and Chicago, Illinois. It was black and has no listed patent numbers. It was the first model. Common. Value: $75.

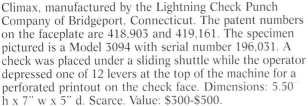

Baby Defiance, manufactured by the Defiance Machine Company, Rochester, New York, which applied for the patent. This was obviously the first model of the Baby Defiance with an ivory-like label on the front of the machine. A wheel on the right hand side indicates the selected amount. To print the amount, the operator needed to punch the top knob down forcefully. Common. Value: $50.

Climax, manufactured by the Lightning Check Punch Company of Bridgeport, Connecticut. The patent numbers on the faceplate are 418,903 and 419,161. The specimen pictured is a Model 3094 with serial number 196,031. A check was placed under a sliding shuttle while the operator depressed one of 12 levers at the top of the machine for a perforated printout on the check face. Dimensions: 5.50" h x 7" w x 5" d. Scarce. Value: $300-$500.

Defiance, manufactured by the Defiance Machine Company, Rochester, New York. This model of the Defiance is very desirable and is considered to be very rare. Its unusual appearance marks it as one of the premier collectibles among check protectors. It was patented on August 6, 1907 and its patent number is 862,844. The clock-like face had 22 key tops that were placed in a circular fashion around a dial. A single handle is used to turn the dial to the desired position. The check is inserted on the right side. A roller at the bottom of the machine was used for inking the slanted printing. The resulting printout was in whole dollars only and had asterisks at beginning and end of the printout, i.e. *FIVE HUNDRED DOLLARS* NOT OVER. Dimensions: 13.50" h x 10" w x 9" d. Rare. Value: $1,000-$1,500.

F & E Checkwriter, manufactured by the Hedman Manufacturing Company, Chicago, Illinois. The pictured unit is a Model A, serial number 160,721. A multiple lever type selector with a hand punch on top. It included an all clear lever for corrections or to clear the mechanism for the next check to be protected. A stenciled message on the lower front of the unit states "Protected by Wm. Burns Detective Agency–International Detective–Original Purchaser Indemnified Against Loss." Dimensions: 10" h x 5" w x 7.50" d. Common. Value: $25.

A later model of the Baby Defiance differs slightly in that the amount wheel has been repositioned to the left side and the hand punch on the top has a leather cushion. It is also shown with the original tube of red indelible ink, which accompanied it when the unit was purchased. It has a patent date of April 13, 1897. It is considered to be readily available. Common. Value: $50-$75.

Dupligraph, manufactured by the Angell Manufacturing Company, Boston, Massachusetts. The machine pictured is a Model A, serial number 1,277. The patent dates are April 2, 1907 and April 9, 1907. The numerals and characters are all displayed on the front of the machine and are accessed by a sliding indicator with a knob on its end, which moved from right to left and also reverses. After selecting the dollar denomination desired, the knob is depressed to punch out the printed amount in an outline of tiny dots. Scarce: Value: $300.

By removing the bottom plate on the F & E Checkwriter, (shown on the preceding page) the operating instructions were clearly available to the operator.

New Era. The following four models of the New Era Check Protector are believed to be Models 2, 3, 4 and 5. The first model pictured is believed to be the Model 2. It is marked only "Patent Pending." The protected amount was stamped on the paper by slapping the top down firmly. Dimensions: 6" h x 3" w x 2" d. Scarce. Value: $75-$125.

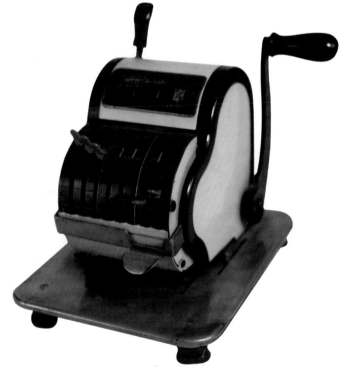

Lightning. This F & E Checkwriter was manufactured by the Hedman Manufacturing Company, Chicago, Illinois. The one pictured is a Series 800, serial number 1,202,247. A later version of the F & E was sold during the 1960s. Common. Value: $25.

New Era, Model 3. The Model 3 was a redesign and used a small hand crank located on the right hand side. The label on this unit designates it as a Model 3, serial number 73,781. Scarce. Value: $50-$75.

New Era, Model 4. The Model 4 is nickel-plated and the hand crank that appeared on the Model 3 has been removed. The serial number is 19,437. After selecting the amount of the check, the top punch was slapped down firmly. This model both prints and perforates. The label reads "Patent Pending." The date of manufacture has been determined to be October 4, 1915. Dimensions: 6.50" h x 6.25" w x 3" d. Scarce. Value: $75-$125.

New Safety, manufactured by the Safety Check Protector Company of Boston, Massachusetts. The front label lists the patent dates of October 29, 1907 and October 12, 1909. The handle is a combination amount selector and punch. It displays a dotted outline of numerals and three characters. Dimensions: 6" h x 4.50" w x 9.50" d. Rare. Value: $300-$500.

New Era, Model 5. The Model 5 is clearly identified on the label on the top. It has two listed patent dates, March 9, 1920 and April 20, 1920. There are two horizontal handles, one on each side of the dial. One was used to select the dollar amount and the other to impress that amount on the check. Scarce. Value: $75-$125.

Page, manufactured by the Page Check Protector Company, San Francisco, California. It lists a patent date of October 1, 1912 and patent number 1,039,789. A small portable hand held check protector that was only 2.75" in diameter. One simply inserted the check between the number and the base of the unit and depressed the figure. The result was a perforated number in a dot pattern. Scarce. Value: $150-$200.

Right and below: Parks, J. B., manufactured by the National Safety Check Punch Company and patented on May 17, 1870. This is the earliest check punch in the author's collection. The check was inserted under a paddle-like device and the operator selected and depressed the appropriate lever at the top of the machine for a perforated printout. There are ten numerals and an asterisk (*). Rare. Value: $500.

Peerless. manufactured by the Todd Protectograph Company, Rochester, New York. The model pictured is a SR (senior) with serial number 82,686. An operating lever swings around a segment and can be depressed when the proper amount is accessed. It prints the amount one word at a time. Scarce. Value: $125.

Protectograph, manufactured by the Todd Protectograph Company, Rochester, New York. The picture shows serial number 654,039. There were four models of the Protectograph. One model, the "Exactly," wrote in a straight line, i.e. EXACTLY 25 CENTS. There was also a "motor operated Exactly Model." Unlike the "Exactly" model, which is considered to be a common find, the motor driven version is difficult to locate. The author has never seen one. Value: $300-$500. There was also a Double Zurich Model, which was the same as the Exactly. The only notable difference was that it printed two words at a time. Common. Value: $35-$75.

Left:
Protectograph Personal Check Writer, manufactured by the Todd Protectograph Company. Rochester, New York. The model pictured is a 1500, serial number 99,241. The inventor of this machine was Walter B. Payne who owns patent number 1,661,384, dated March 6, 1928. Judging by the number of these machines that are found in flea markets, it must have been one of the most popular check writers ever manufactured. Dimensions: 5" h x 5.50" w x 3.50" d. Common. Value: $25 approximately.

Royal, manufactured by the Rouse Manufacturing Company, New York, New York and patented by Louis T. Weiss of Brooklyn, New York. The patent number is 603,416, dated May 3, 1898. The inventor claimed that his design was an improvement because the "numbers and other characters could be placed at any desired or convenient place on the check, and would feed the check accurately and forward in a straight line." Dimensions: 4.5" h x 5.50" in diameter. Scarce. Value: $125.

S & P, manufactured by the Sittman & Pitt Company, Brooklyn, New York. The inventors are shown as Walter H. Pitt and Gustav Sittman with a patent number of 534,404, dated February 19, 1895. A rotating lever spins around a circle of numbers from 0 to 9, and by depressing the lever at the desired point a number is punched in a dot pattern on the check. This action also causes the check to advance the proper distance between numbers. Scarce. Value: $125.

Safe-Guard, manufactured by the Safeguard Check Writer Company, Inc. at their factory in Lansdale, Pennsylvania. The pictured machine is a Model S, serial number 146,176. There are four patents stenciled on the machine, January 16, 1917; March 6, 1917; July 10, 1917, and October 8, 1918. Amounts were imprinted in words diagonally across the check. Numeral selection was achieved by using combination hand wheel and dial located on the left side of the machine. Depression of the operating handle caused impression and its return to the original position to advance the paper. Common. Value: $25.

Safe-Guard Instant, manufactured by the Safeguard Check Writer Company at their factory in Lansdale, Pennsylvania. It states simply "Patent Pending." The instant model was a lever setting type in which the payee's name was protected by shredding a pattern over it. There were several models of the Instant. Common. Value: $35.

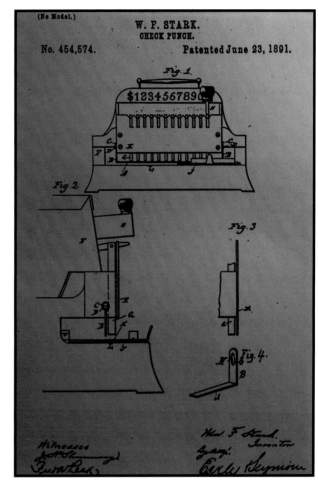

Above and left:
Standard Automatic Safety Punch, manufactured by the Hoggson & Pettis Manufacturing Company, New Haven, Connecticut. The pictured unit had patents dated May 10, 1887; July 24, 1888, and June 23, 1891 and a serial number of 4,995. The patentee, William Stark claimed that the object of his invention was to prevent the paper or checks from being crumpled or torn. An index lever was moved to the number selected and depressed to cause that number to be perforated on the check. Dimensions: 6" h x 10" w x 5" d. Rare. Value: $400-$600.

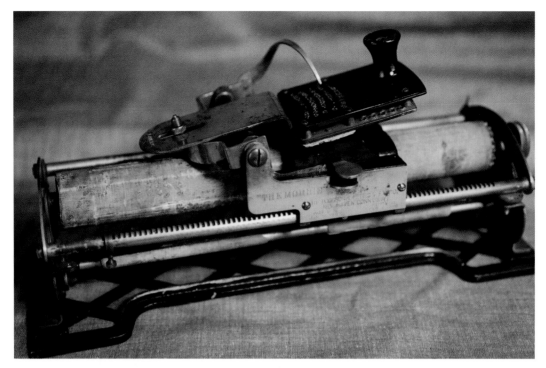

Morris. The manufacturer of Standard Automatic Safety Punch also manufactured this very collectible typewriter. Rare. Value: $8,000+.

Todd Junior, manufactured by the Todd Company, Inc., Rochester, New York. Pictured is the Model 2. First patent number is 1,030,690 and the last patent number is 1,673,162. This machine was a six column, lever type set up with a visible window display or readout. Dimensions: 5" h x 4.50" w x 6" d. Common. Value: $35.

Todd Electric, manufactured by the Todd Company, Inc. of Rochester, New York. This heavy-duty electric check protector weighs 45 pounds. It is a seven column, push button type with a repeat and clear key. There are 42 patent numbers listed on the back of the machine with the first being patent number 1,864,941 and the last 2,092,862. Dimensions: 8" h x 15" w x 10" d. Scarce. Value: $50-$75.

United States Check Punch, manufactured by the United States Check Punch Company, Newark, New Jersey. The serial number of the pictured machine is 2,008. The machine has three patent dates listed, May 29, 1888; October 22, 1889; and December 8, 1891. Charles A. Randall of New York was the inventor. A single lever is used to select and activate the cutters, which the inventor claimed eliminated the need for a series of levers or dials. It is housed in an attractive oak case and has gold decorative stenciling on the front of the machine. Dimensions: 7" h x 7.75" w x 6" d. Common. Value: $125.

Left and above:
Wesley, manufactured by the Wesley Manufacturing Company, New York, New York. Invented by Charles E. Ongley of New York who applied for and received patent number 584,518 on June 15, 1897. A series of needles perforated the check, then impressed an inkpad and returned to ink the perforation. Scarce. Value: $75-$125.

Universal, manufactured by the Universal Manufacturing Company, Boston, Massachusetts. A large handle acts as both the selector and the punch lever, by twisting the handle and selecting a numeral from 1 to 9 or the symbols "*" or "$." Scarce. Value: $300.

# CHAPTER V
# COPIERS, DUPLICATORS AND DICTATION

## COPIERS

As early as the year 1648, an English inventor, Sir William Petty, patented an "instrument for writing many copies at once." However, in practice it was found to take more time to copy a letter than to write it twice.

More than 125 years later, the distinguished inventor, James Watt of Birmingham, England would apply his skills at developing a solution to the problem of writing letters twice to retain a copy.

A friend of Watt, Dr. Charles Darwin, suggested that he invent a device for copying letters. Darwin used the example of possibly a duplex pen, which he called a biographer, perhaps similar to Sir William Petty's 1648 invention.

The idea intrigued Watt and in 1775 after much trial and error, he developed a device which he called a "rolling pin press." Many experiments were exhausted before he found suitable ink that would provide sharp and durable copies without hurting the original.

Watt's "Copy Press" patent drawing, patent date: February 14, 1780.

PLATE II.

The drawing, Fig. 1st represents a Front, or end View, of the Rolling Prefs invented by me and referred to in the above specification. A.B.C. is one of the ends of an Iron or Wooden Frame which serves to connect the two Rollers. D.D. are two wooden or metalline Rollers, turned extremely exact, or truely Cylindrical, and which are mounted on Iron Axles firmly fixt in them. E.E. is a double ended Lever, by means of which the Roller on whose Axle it is applied may be forcibly turned round. F.F. represents the Board of the Rolling Prefs on which the writings to be copied are to be laid. N.N. is a piece of Cloth or other elastic pliable substance placed next the Roller and above the writings to be Copied, and the board. G. is a strong plank of wood or plate of metal serving to connect the two end pieces of the frame at Bottom. H.H. represents the edge of a common table to which the Prefs may be fastened by the Iron Screw Cramps J.J. K is a slitt, of which there is one in each end piece of the frame, these slitts are filled with elastic steel, or other metalline springs, or with some other elastic substances, which serve to prefs the two Rolls forcibly together L is a Brafs Bolster, supported upon the springs, and serving to support the end of the axis of the under Roller. The Drawing Fig. 2d represents a side view of the Rolling Prefs, in which AB. AB. are the two end pieces of the frame D.D. are the two Rollers. E is the double ended Lever. G is the strong plank or Plate of metal which forms the bottom of the Frame. H.H. is the table on which the Prefs stands. J. is one of the Iron Cramps which fasten the Prefs to the table, and M. is a Barr of Iron which connects the upper part of the frame. Fig. 3d represents a screw Prefs which may be used instead of the Rolling Prefs in taking off imprefsions from writings. AA is a double ended Lever. BB The Screw, C. a block of wood or metal, which the screw acts upon, and which is attached to it. DD. the frame of the Prefs made of Iron or wood. EE a moveable board, on which the writing to be copied is to be laid with a cloth over it. FF. the Bottom or Sole of the prefs made of wood or metal. Be it remembered that these Prefses are made of different sizes according to the sizes or largenefses of the writings intended to be copied. Those drawn above are drawn from one sufficiently large to take an imprefsion from a folio page of writing on Post Paper, and are drawn to a scale of one inch and a half for each foot, or one eighth of their natural Size.

Watt's "Copy Press" patent text

Watt described his invention by stating that "the greatest part of the secret resides in the *mechanical manoeuvre!* The original letter to be copied, enterleafed with same, unsized copying-paper and oil paper or pasteboard; to pressure for a few seconds between the rollers of a rolling press; or in fact any adequate and equable pressure, not too powerful; so that the ink may be duly impressed on the copy without being forced through the letter paper, so as to injure the appearance of the letter."

Watt's invention proved to be practical and he began manufacturing copiers through his firm, James Watt and Company.

Twenty years later, in 1800, his son, James Watt, Jr. recognized the need for a more portable copier for people traveling. He created and patented a portable copier, using the same rolling press principle.

Watt Portable Copier. Dimensions: 11.75" w x 17.5" long x 5.25" d. Rare. Value: $3,000.

Although Watt Sr. preferred to use the rolling press principle, he stated that "as an alternative to the *rolling press,* one could use a *screw type press.*" The screw type press caught on with the end-users and became very popular for many years.

The following picture is an example of the screw type press.

H. B. Company copier press was exhibited at the World's Columbia Exhibition and at the Cotton States Exposition where premium awards were won. (c.1893) Scarce. Value: $150.

## DUPLICATORS

For multiple copies, the Mimeograph, invented by Thomas A. Edison and patented August 8, 1876, became a universal standard for businesses of that period. The medium used was called a stencil. Stencils are sheets of tough fibrous tissue that is treated with a patented formula to make the surface ink resistant.

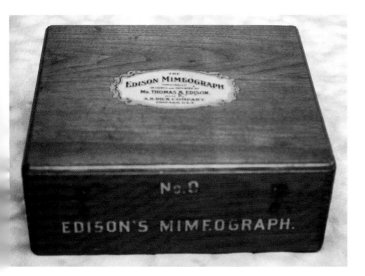

Left and above:
Edison Mimeograph, Model No. 0, manufactured by the A.B. Dick Company, Chicago, Illinois. Patented by Thomas A. Edison. (c.1880) Dimensions: 13" w x 11" long x 5" d. Value: $150.

Above and right:
Edison Mimeograph, Model No. 1, manufactured by the A.B. Dick Company, Chicago, Illinois. First patent date: August 8, 1876, last patent date: February 17, 1880. Dimensions: 17" w x 13.25" long x 4.75" d. Value: $200.

Left and above:
Remington Red-Seal Duplicator, manufactured by E. Remington & Sons, Ilion, New York. It has a very low serial number: 101. Dimensions: 20.25" w x 15.25" long x 6.25" d. Rare. Value: $500.

Underwood Standard Duplicator, manufactured by the Underwood Typewriter Company, Inc., New York, New York. Dimensions: 19.5" w x 15.5" long x 6.25" d. Scarce. Value: $200.

Mimeograph No. 75, manufactured by the A.B. Dick Company, Chicago, Illinois. First patent date: June 30, 1903. Last patent date: February 2, 1904. Serial Number: 30,784. Value: $150.

Mimeograph No. 72 (portable), manufactured by the A.B. Dick Company, Chicago, Illinois. First patent date: February 24, 1915. Last patent date: October 9, 1928. Value: $75.

Above and left:
Edison Rotary Mimeograph No. 76, manufactured by the A.B. Dick Company, Chicago, Illinois. First patent date: June 22, 1897. Last patent date: January 9, 1906. Value: $125.

Above and right:
Underwood Revolving Duplicator, manufactured by the
Underwood Typewriter Company, New York, New York.
(c.1925) Value: $50.

Rotospeed Duplicator, manufactured by the
Rotospeed Company, Dayton, Ohio. (c.1925)
Value: $50.

## DICTATION

In 1876, Alexander Graham Bell set up the Volta Laboratory in Washington. D.C.. The laboratory was named after the Volta prize money of $10,000 that the French government had recently awarded Bell. Bell and his cousin Chichester Bell and Charles Sumner Tainter formed the original staff at the new laboratory.

**Chichester Bell**

**Alexander Graham Bell**

## Charles Sumner Tainter

The Graphaphone

One of the early participants in Bell and Tainter's new firm was Edward D. Easton who was an official congressional reporter. Easton found it more convenient to dictate his notes directly into the recorder as soon as he left the House of Representatives. With the Graphaphone, a typist could easily transcribe his dictation. As a result of Easton's application and the enthusiasm of the other congressional reporters, Tainter rented space from the Howe Sewing Machine Company in Bridgeport, Connecticut to start production of the first dictating machine. The sewing machine treadle powered these early models, just as it did on the typewriter.

Their first project was to develop a device to record sound for use with the newly invented telephone. On October 17, 1881, they submitted to the Smithsonian Institute the results of their work, "a device which had a rotating cardboard drum coated with a 50-50 mixture of beeswax and plain paraffin. The mouthpiece has a diaphragm not unlike that used in Bell's telephone. Attached to the diaphragm was a concave steel stylus which vibrated up and down in the same degree as the diaphragm."

On October 5, 1881, Tainter tested the device for the first time and picked up the mouthpiece and recited a quotation from Shakespeare's "Hamlet," "There are more things in heaven and earth, Horatio, than are dreamt of in your philosophy." As Tainter was speaking, he manually hand cranked the device, which turned a drum at an appropriate speed to cut this historic recording. Tainter used a doctor's stethoscope to listen to the playback. At that point, a business dictating device had been invented and was later called a "Graphaphone."

Graphaphone on a sewing machine stand powered by the treadle

The first machines were called "Commercial Graphaphones," but use of the word "commercial" was frowned upon; especially in England. The British preferred the name "dictaphone" instead. The name caught on and eventually became synonymous with this type of device. The Dictaphone Company today is a division of Pitney-Bowes.

Dictaphone Shaving Machine Model 7, Type S, manufactured by the Columbia Graphaphone Company, New York. A shaving machine was used to scrape previous etchings off the wax cylinder so that it could be reused for new dictation. Rare. Value: $100.

Dictaphone Model 7 Type B, manufactured by the Columbia Graphaphone Company, New York. Serial Number: 32,978. First patent date: October 16,1894. Last patent date: September 13, 1910. Rare. Value: $200.

Dictaphone Model 10, manufactured by the Dictaphone Corporation, Bridgeport, Connecticut. Serial Number: 102,095. Scarce. Value: $75.

Edison Business Phonograph, manufactured by the Thomas A. Edison Company, Orange, New Jersey. Serial Number: 8,264C. First patent date: June 20, 1900. Last patent date: May 22, 1906. Rare. Value: $300.

Executive Ediphone, manufactured by the Thomas A. Edison Company, West Orange, New Jersey. This model was awarded the Grand Prize at the Sesquicentennial in 1926. Serial Number: 274,812. First patent number: 1,106,338. Last patent number: 1,615,114.

Edison (Pyrotechnic) Voicewriter, manufactured by the Thomas A. Edison Company, West Orange, New Jersey. Value: $150.

Edison Voicewriter Model 86000, manufactured by the Thomas A. Edison Company, West Orange, New Jersey. Serial Number: 20,469. Value: $75

# CHAPTER VI
# MEDALS, AWARDS, NOVELTIES AND TOYS

Industry related awards, medals and buttons, such as service and anniversary pins, are attractive treasures for collectors of office related technologies. They are collected not only by office machine collectors, but also by those who are interested in advertising and toys. The size of these items generally does not create a storage problem for a collector and the availability of new and unique items seems endless. The Remington Typewriter Company of Ilion, New York is one example of an office machine manufacturer who recognized the benefit of medals and awards. They felt it was an attractive way to recognize their employees and customers.

Around the turn of the century, the Remington Typewriter Company was one of the first large manufacturers to recognize the benefits of an Employee Relations Program to enhance the morale and *esprit de corps* of their workers. In 1906, one of the eight departments within the Remington Typewriter Company was the Labor Department. This department was in charge of a group called "Industrial Betterment," which was responsible for seeing that loyal employees were properly rewarded. Some of the methods used were gold dollar bonuses, certificates, and service pins, such as are pictured on the following pages.

## MEDALS

Service pin (gold), Remington Typewriter Company, 5 years of service. Value: $100.

Service pin (gold), Remington Typewriter Company, 15 years of service. Value: $150.

Service pin (gold), Remington Typewriter Company, 25 years of service. Value: $200.

Service pin (gold), Remington Typewriter Company, 10 years of service. Value: $100.

Service pin (gold), Remington Typewriter Company, 20 years of service. Value: $200.

Service pin (gold), Remington Typewriter Company, 35 years of service. Value: $300.

Service pin (gold), "WSB" Remington Typewriter Company, 10 years of service. Notice the "WSB" which stood for Wyckoff, Seamans and Benedict. They purchased the Remington Typewriter Company in 1882 from E. Remington & Sons. The author has located only two examples of their service pins to date. Value: $150.

Service pin (gold), "WSB" Remington Typewriter Company, 15 years of service. Value: $125.

75th Anniversary pin. In 1926, Jim Rand purchased the Remington Typewriter Company from Wyckoff, Seamans and Benedict and formed the Remington Rand Corporation. In the same year, Remington Rand distributed the 75th Anniversary pin depicting the Remington Typewriter. Value: $150.

Left and below:
Anniversary watch fob. Remington Arms, the first manufacturer of the Remington typewriter, issued a commemorative watch fob in 1916, marking the 100th Anniversary of the Remington Arms Company. Pictured on the side of the medallion is the first log cabin forge where Eliphalet Remington made his first rifle. Below it is a picture of the 1916 Remington Arms factory, and below that is a picture of the typewriter as it played a significant part in the company history. Value: $100.

Speed typing medals and certificates were developed by the Remington Typewriter Company for those students who achieved a degree of proficiency in the "touch method" of typing. Typing proficiency medals. Value each: $10-$15.

Remington's first typewriter was named after the inventors, Sholes and Glidden. It was first placed on the market in 1873. In 1973, on the Remington Typewriter's 100th Anniversary, this award was presented to all Remington dealers who achieved 100% of their annual sales quota. It is not known how many were made, but it is estimated at between 200 and 300. Movable parts included the foot pedal and carriage. The author is not aware of any being sold, and therefore its value is an estimate. Value: $500.

Remington Awards Program booklet. Value: $40.

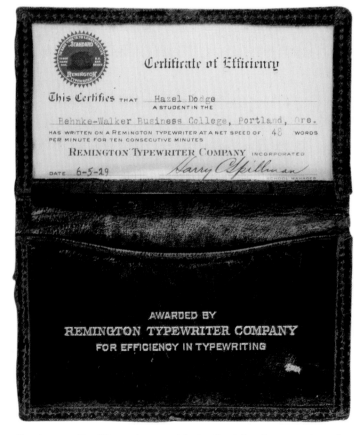

Remington Certificate (encased in leather) for the operator who achieved a certain degree of proficiency. Value: $40.

A medal developed to reward those typists who could type 55 net words per minute. Value: $25.

Above and above right:
Underwood medal for typing proficiency. Value: $25.

Left:
Underwood Typewriter awards program booklet. Value: $35.

Right:
Remington Typewriter Company Field Day award for the "Hammer Throw Contest" awarded on June 3, 1906. Value: $40.

## NOVELTIES

IBM Selectric typing element (1.25" in diameter) next to larger version that is a paper clip holder (3" in diameter). Value: $15.

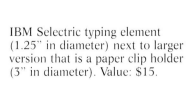

Royal Typewriter paper clip holder, "Regal Typewriter Company, Inc., 75 Varich Street, New York." Regal Typewriter was a typewriter rebuilding facility. (c.1930) Dimensions: 3.50" x 4.25". Value: $125.

Royal Typewriter paper clip holder. (c.1960). Value: $75.

R.C. Allen Typewriter paper weight. Dimensions: 2.75" x 3". Value: $50.

Panasonic Typewriter calculator, made in China (c.1990). Dimensions: 3.5" x 3". Value: $15.

North Pole typewriter (Christmas tree ornament), NPT Shire Printing Company, 1993, Enesco. Designed by Lustre Fame, LTD and made in China. Dimensions: 3" x 1.75". Value: $8.

Crystal typewriter by Swarovski entitled "Crystal Memories," made in Austria (c.1990). Value: $35.

Porcelain typewriter jewelry box, Lemoge, France. Hand painted by Rochard. Dimensions: 1.75" x 2.25". (c.1990) Value: $25.

Typewriter cigarette lighters in two different sizes. Value each: $50.

Desk and typewriter salt & pepper shakers. Marked S.D.D. © 1988, Five & Dime, Inc., division of Sarsaparilla, Made in Korea. Dimensions: Desk, 2" x 4"; typewriter, 2.5" x 1.25". Value: $20.

Dear Santa teapot shaped like a typewriter with miniature Santa's Helpers. Value: $10.

Ceramic teapot shaped like a typewriter & desk. Made by Garden Design in England. Dimensions: 12" x 4". Value: $45.

Typewriter with kitten, made in Japan. Dimensions: 2" x 3". Value: $10.

Jim Beam typewriter and computer. Genuine Regal China Corporation, 145-liquor bottle, 1984 Republican National Campaign. Dimensions: 7.5" x 6". Value: $30.

Tip trays, Globe Warnicke Office Furniture and
L. C. Smith Brothers Typewriter. Value each: $50.

Deck of playing cards depicting Elliott
Addressing Company factory and
products. Value: $20.

Bookends awarded by
L. C. Smith & Corona
Typewriter Company.
Value: $75.

Three paperweights by National Cash Register, Remington Rand and Caligraph Typewriter Company. Values respectively: $35; $25; and $75.

Remington Rand Typewriter Corporation cuff links and key chain. Value for set: $50.

IBM memo pad with the word "THINK" engraved in gold, (c.1950). Value: $15.

Lady's hat pin by Hammond Typewriter Company. Value; $125.

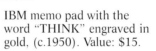

Monarch Typewriter memo pad in which one could make pencil notes and, after erasing them, reuse the pad. Value: $35.

Magnifying glass, IBM Field Engineering Awards Conference, 1969 in Denver, Colorado. Value: $25.

Electric National Cash Register digital clock, calendar and jewelry box. (c.1938) Value: $120.

Rulers & paper clip. Marchant Calculator and Noiseless Typewriter Ruler. Value each: $20. Houston Typewriter Exchange paper clip. Value: $5.

Two paperweights depicting R.C. Allen adding machines, one a full keyboard unit and the other a 10-key Adder. (c.1950) Value each: $35.

Paperweight of first cash register
entitled "The Ritty," later to become the
National Cash Register. Value: $175.

Occupational shaving mug with early model typewriter.
(c.1890) Value: $500.

Replica of the first Xerox copier mounted on
commemorative wood grained base. Value: $150.

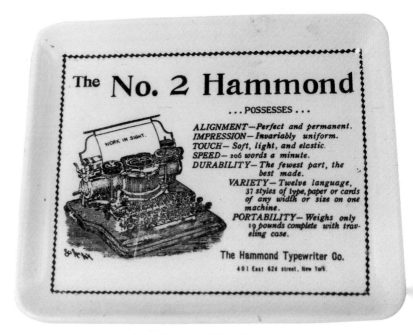

Ash tray with picture of the Hammond No. 2
Typewriter. (c.1890) Value: $35.

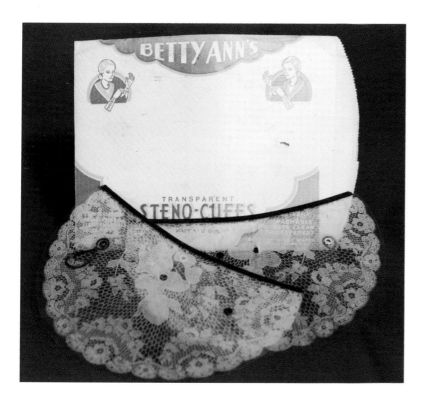

Cigarette lighter, APSCO. Value: $20.

Stapler, Raggedy Ann. Value: $35.

Left:
Lady's Steno Cuffs labeled "Betty Anns." Value: $50.

Teapot desk with cash register and typewriter. Value: $35.

Pottery typists, no markings. Value: $5.

115

Barclay toy soldier typist. (c.1946) Value: $165.

Typewriter bank, "My Own Typewriter Bank," Ardee. Dimensions: 4" X 3.50". Value: $25.

Typewriter banks "1939 Worlds Fair, New York," Remington Rand Electrical Products Pavilion. These souvenirs were available in gold, silver, and black. Dimensions: 2.5" x 2.5". Value: $50-$70.

Typewriter bank, Underwood, New York World's Fair. (c.1940) Gold painted. Dimensions: 2.50" x 2.75". Value: $50-$75.

Wood toy typewriter atop a jewelry box, plays musical tune "The Syncopated Clock" when the drawer is opened. Made in Japan. Value: $35.

Typewriter bank, IBM Model D; Durham Industries, New York, New York. Made in Hong Kong. Dimensions: 5.25" x 4.5". Value: $25.

Toy mechanical typist and typewriters entitled "The Typist" and "Miss Busy Bee" respectively. Value each: $125.

"Miss Friday" mechanical
toy typewriter. Value: $200.

Mechanical toy typewriter "Tom Thumb." Value: $25.

Kiddie Toy Cash Register, manufactured by the
Cleveland Metal Stamping Company. (No. 100)
Value: $50.

# CHAPTER VII
# PENCIL SHARPENERS

From the time the pencil was first introduced, along with all the benefits it offered, one problem persisted: how to keep it sharpened. A technique soon surfaced. All you needed was a penknife to whittle away the wood until a point was made that was suitable for writing. Some companies, such as Remington, offered a small office knife for just that purpose. But the need for a better solution was obvious.

The *Scientific American Magazine* of December 20, 1913 described a device that could save time; should not waste the pencil by cutting more than was necessary; should do neat work; should not create a mess from shavings; and should not require a special skill.

Among the solutions developed were four basic types. One was a reciprocating device similar to a chisel. A second was similar to a whittler. It actually whittled away the wood in the same way a person would with a penknife. A third was the sand paper or rasp file type. The fourth was the small beveled milling cutter type, available with one, two, and three-sided milling cutters.

In recent years, the interest and value of the earlier pencil sharpeners (sometimes called pencil pointers) have skyrocketed. Some of these devices will continue to be a good investment for collectors.

Cincinnati pencil sharpener, manufactured by the Cincinnati Pump Company. A patent was applied for. It was a mill-type pencil sharpener that was created to resemble a "Water Thrifter," a product marketed by the Cincinnati Pump Company. Dimensions: 11" h x 8.5" w x 10.5" d. Value: $300-$400.

Angell pencil sharpener, manufactured by the Angell Company, Boston, Massachusetts. The Angell is a whittler-type pencil sharpener. By turning the handle, the mechanism allows two circular blades to travel in an up and down motion. At the same time turning the pencil to allow the sharpener to evenly whittle away the wood surrounding the lead. Dimensions: 4.25" h x 2.25" w x 5.50" d. Rare. Value: $500.

Coffee grinder pencil sharpener. The origin of these coffee grinder pencil sharpeners is unknown to the author. Each one has an Eagle decal on its side. It is considered to be a common find. Dimensions: 5.5" h x 5.8" w and 3 ¾" d. Value: $25-$50.

Cohen, B.S., a small pencil pointer encased in a wood tube as a case., It is marked that it was patented September 2, 1879 in London, England. Scarce. Value: $75-$100.

Dux. A small brass pencil pointer marked as a Model 145 with a three position knob. A single blade shaved the pencil to a degree of sharpness that was indicated by the three positions. It came with its own leather carrying case. Dimensions: 1.125" h x .4375" w x .5" d. Common. Value: $25-$50.

Ellison, J.B. This unit was patented August 18, 1908 and was a small desktop pencil pointer or shaver. It has a single blade. The top is removable by a screw-like knob on one end of the device. Under the name, J.B. Ellison & Sons, is imprinted the name "Woolens." Dimensions: 1.5" h x 2" w and 3.5" d. Scarce. Value: $150-$200.

Esco, Automatic Screw Cutting Pencil Sharpener, manufactured by Tailhade & Ronselli Unicos Importadores, Reconquista 258, Rivadavia/1015 of Buenos Aires, Argentina. The Esco is a desk model single mill machine. Scarce. Value: $125-$175.

Right:
Evalast Pencil Pointer. A display for retail counter tops containing twelve (12) pencil pointers per sheet. Each pointer has rasp-like sides with a sharp edge at one end similar to a chisel. Dimensions: .75" h x 4.50" w. Scarce. Value (per display sheet): $150-$200.

Below:
Gem. A unique sandpaper type sharpener. As the handle was turned it activated two gears that turned the sharpening wheel. Manufactured by Gould & Cook, Leominster, Massachusetts. It was issued patent number 342,350 on May 25, 1886 to its inventors, Charles E. Gould and Frank H. Cook. Rare. Value: $500.

Graffco pencil sharpener, manufactured by the Graff-Underwood Company at 14 Beacon Street, Somerville Station, Boston, Massachusetts. It was a single mill-type sharpener with a nickel-plated cover. Dimensions: 7" h x 4" diameter. Common. Value: $125.

Grantzon pencil sharpener, invented by E. Grantzon and covered by patent number 1,075,971 dated October 14, 1913. This is a six (6) blade whittler that works in a similar fashion to the Right and the U.S. pencil sharpeners. Common. Value: $150.

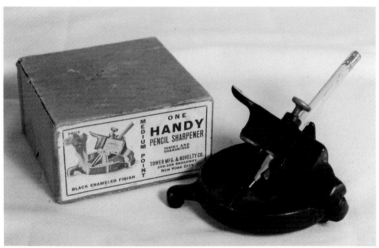

Handy pencil sharpener, manufactured by the Tower Manufacturing and Novelty Company at 306-308 Broadway, New York, New York. A shaver-type with a single blade with which you whittled away at the pencil point. It is shown with its original carrying case/box. Dimensions: 2" h x 4.25" diameter. Scarce. Value: $250.

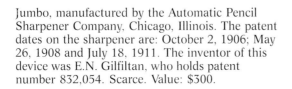

Jumbo, manufactured by the Automatic Pencil Sharpener Company, Chicago, Illinois. The patent dates on the sharpener are: October 2, 1906; May 26, 1908 and July 18, 1911. The inventor of this device was E.N. Gilfiltan, who holds patent number 832,054. Scarce. Value: $300.

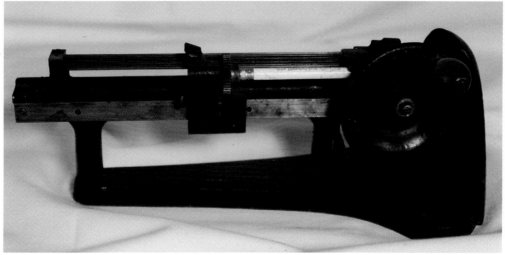

Jupiter, manufactured in Hamburg, Germany by the Guhl and Harbeck Company. The A.B. Dick Company marketed it in the United States. The original inventor was Heinrich August Hermann Guhl and he holds patent number 830,662, dated September 11, 1906. These are examples of models 1 and 2 respectively. Scarce. Value: $500-$600.

Keep-A-Point, manufactured by the Portable Machinery Company, Patent Pending. A small single blade-type in which the operator twisted or turned the pencil while the blade shaved off the wood tip. Dimensions: 1.75" h x 2" w x 1.75" d. Common. Value: $35.

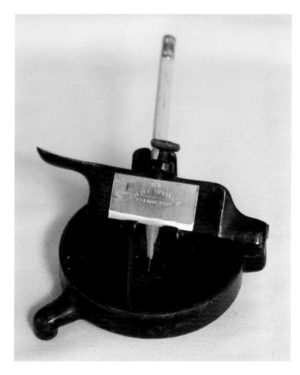

Little Shaver, patented on March 19, 1904. The Little Shaver is a whittler-type. The pencil is held in one hand and with the other hand a handle is depressed. The handle has a single blade attached to it. When the pencil is turned a stroke of the blade shaves off a small sliver of wood and sharpens the pencil. Scarce. Value: $200.

124

Right:
Myers, Louis, manufactured by the Mechanical Products Company, Brooklyn, New York. It was patented on November 12, 1912. It has four (4) settings for fine, medium, coarse and crayon. Dimensions: 5" h x 3.5" w x 3.74" d. Scarce. Value: $200.

New Era, manufactured by the New Era Manufacturing Company, New York, New York with patent pending. The serial number of the pictured machine is 30,400. The New Era pencil sharpener was a whittler-type. The operator had to push the handle up and down, which caused a wheel-like knife to shave the wood away from the pencil point. Dimensions: 6.5" h x 2" w x 2" d. Scarce. Value: $200.

Peerless Whittler (A), Two Blade, manufactured by the Burke Manufacturing Company, New York, New York. Turning the handle caused the two blades to rotate and shave the wood from the pencil tip. Dimensions: 6" h x 3" w x 4" d. Rare. Value: $400.

Peerless Whittler (B), Three Blade, manufactured by the Peerless Whittler Company, New York, New York. The Model B had three (3) sharp blades. It is the same as the Model A Two Blade version except it had triple cutters. Rare. Value: $500.

Pencil cutter & sharpener, manufactured by "Papeterie Marion" of Paris, France. Its patent is registered under the following dates: September 5, 1851; October 6 & 7, Vic. Very early pencil sharpener with an ivory handle, shown in its original box. Also included is the original operating instructions. Rare. Value: $500.

Perfect Pencil Pointer, manufactured by the E.S. Drake Pencil Sharpener Company, 105 Middle Street, Portland, Maine. The inventor, Edwin S. Drake patented the unit on April 29, 1890 under patent number 426,716. The Perfect Pencil Pointer was also marketed by the Goodell Company of Antrium, New Hampshire. The user held a spindle-like carriage holding the pencil against the rasp file with one hand and the pencil was moved back and forth as it was sharpened. Rare. Value: $250.

Above and right:
Planetary Pencil Pointer, manufactured by the A.B. Dick Company, 152-154 Lake Street, Chicago, Illinois and 47 Nassau Street, New York, New York. It was patented on March 17, 1896. The Planetary uses a system of wheel cutters that were turned by bevel cogs. The Planetary was designed to be used either on a desk or fastened to the wall. Dimensions: 5.75" h x 6.50" w x 3.75" d. Scarce. Value: $75.

Quick Pencil Sharpener, manufactured by the
Progress Office Specialty Company, Inc., 72 Spring
Street, New York, New York. It was patented on
August 27, 1909 and the inventor was Louis Myers.
Dimensions: 5" h x 3.25" w x 3" d. Scarce. Value:
$200.

Right Pencil Sharpener, manufactured by the Everett
Specialty Company, New York, New York. This device has a
three blade sharpener that whittled away the pencil as a
crank is turned. Scarce. Value: $175.

Roneo, Automatic Screw Cutting Pencil Sharpener,
manufactured by the Roneo Company, 371 Broadway, New
York, New York. The Roneo uses a spiral cutter or milling
device. There are eight cutting surfaces. The pencils are
automatically gripped and fed. Scarce. Value: $75.

Roneo No. 6, manufactured by Roneo Company, 371
Broadway, New York, New York. The same cutting mechanism
is used on previous models. Rare. Value: $700.

Simplicia, manufactured by Ideal, D.R.G.M. of
Germany. A six blade whittler-type pencil
sharpener. It was invented by E. Grantzon and
carries patent number 1,075,971 dated October
14, 1913. Dimensions: 5.50" h x 4" w x 3.50" d.
Value: $200.

S B Pencil Sharpener.
The pictured model is
serial number 4,042.
Dimensions: 5" h x
13" w x 4.75" d.
Scarce. Value: $325.

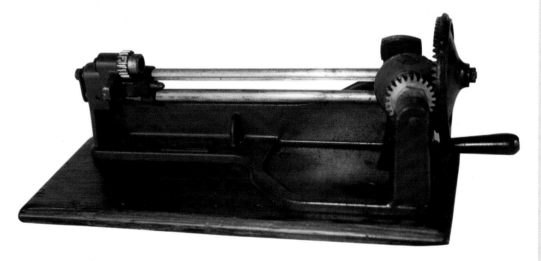

Star Lead Pencil Sharpener, manufactured by the Star Novelty Company, 209 N. 6th Street, Reading, Pennsylvania. The Star Pencil Sharpener with its original box pictured above was a primitive knife cutter-type that was more a novelty than an effective office sharpener. Rare. Value: $250.

U.S. Automatic, manufactured by the Automatic Pencil Sharpener Company, Inc., New York, New York. The U.S. Automatic was a very popular pencil sharpener that was a whittler-type with three (3) blades. Dimensions: 4.75" x 3" w. Common. Value: $175.

Victor. The Victor is the same sharpener as the Planetary, but marketed by the Victor Company. Scarce. Value: $125.

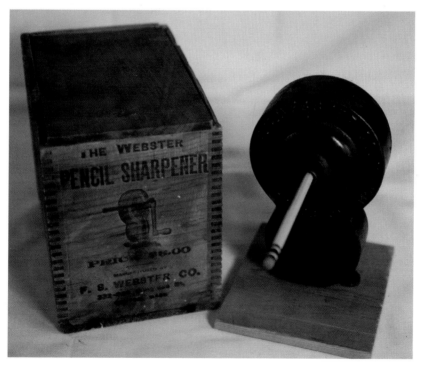

Webster, manufactured by the F.S. Webster Company with offices in New York, New York, Boston, Massachusetts, and Chicago, Illinois. It was patented on June 21, 1892 and May 1, 1900. Dimensions: 7" h x 4.25" w x 4" d. Scarce. Value: $125.

## Figural Pencil Sharpeners

Pictured below are 19 models of figural pencil sharpeners. They are small single blade pencil sharpeners and were designed primarily for use by school children. They were usually carried in their pencil boxes. They were made in a variety of figures, such as: automobiles, guns, the Statue of Liberty, etc. The following is a sampling of these figural sharpeners. Their availability and value are listed in each caption.

Cannon, Germany. Scarce. Value: $65.

Cement mixer, Hong Kong. Scarce. Value: $50.

Bingo pencil sharpener. Scarce. Value: $35.

Tin car, Japanese. Scarce. Value: $50.

Clown, manufactured by KUM of West Germany. D B Patent D. B. G. M. Angel–red design. Scarce. Value: $75.

Red car, Japanese. Scarce. Value: $50.

Dixon pencil sharpener. manufactured by E. Faber Company of New York, New York. Common. Value: $25.

George Washington,
Bicentennial Celebration
1732 to 1932. Scarce.
Value: $75.

Gold hummingbird, has dual opening for
either a pencil or a crayon. Rare.
Value: $90.

Gun (gold). Dimensions: 2.50" long x 1.75"
h. Rare. Value: $75.

Gun (red). Dimensions: 2.25" long x 2.50"
h. Rare. Value: $75.

Janus # 4046, A.W. Faber
of Germany. Common.
Value: $25.

Jeep (small red), Japanese.
Dimensions: .75" long x 1" h
x 1" w. Rare. Value: $95.

Milk bottle key chain
pencil sharpener.
Common. Value: $25.

Motorcycle.
Scarce.
Value: $45.

Student Sharpener, patent dated
December 11, 1906. Common.
Value: $25.

Statue of Liberty.
Rare. Value: $90.

Blow torch. Rare. Value:
$85.

Trumpet, Germany.
Rare. Value: $75.

# CHAPTER VIII

# TIME CLOCKS
# AND TOY TYPEWRITERS

Time clocks are collected by horologists and office technology enthusiasts. The primary function of these devices is to record employee attendance. Each employee checked in and out. The device recorded how long he or she was at work. Late arrivals and overtime were usually printed in red.

Some of these devices were very sophisticated and not only recorded the employee's in and out status and overtime, but also computed each employee's earnings based on individual hourly rates. Deductions for taxes were made. They were capable of computing the total take home pay for as many as 300 employees for each machine and in addition provided a complete payroll journal.

## TIME CLOCKS

Bundy Time Clock, manufactured by the W. H. Bundy Recording Company, Binghamton, New York. First patented June 2, 1885, and last patented November 3, 1897. Value: $700.

Calculagraph, manufactured by the Calculagraph Company, 50 Church Street, New York, New York. The Calculagraph was an elapsed time recorder. It printed the elapsed time between the start and finish of a project. (c.1928) Value: $150.

Cincinnati, manufactured by the Cincinnati Time Recorder Company, Cincinnati, Ohio. Pictured Model is a Series No. 27. (c.1928) It could automatically shift from in to out, or from day to day. Value: $500.

Dey Workmen's Time Recorder (Floor Model), manufactured by the Dey Time Register Company, Syracuse, New York. Inventor: John Dey of Syracuse, New York. Patent number: 524,102, November 11, 1892. It computed payroll based on hours worked and deductions. (c.1892) Value: $800.

Dey Time Clock (Wall Model), manufactured by the Dey Time Register Company, Syracuse, New York. Time in and time out model. (c.1900) Value: $300.

Globe Time Clock, manufactured by W.A. Wood, Montreal, Canada. This was a weekly time register. The top dial recorded each day of the week. (c.1920) Value: $1,000.

International Time Recorder (Floor Model), manufactured by International Business Machines Corporation, Time Recording Division, Endicott, New York. Model 6135 was a weekly, 2-color record; with capacity for 100 employees; 6 registrations daily for 7 days. (c.1928) Value (with original stand): $1,200.

International Time Recorder (Floor Model) internal mechanism.

International Time Clock (Wall Model), manufactured by International Business Machines Corporation, Time Recording Division, Endicott, New York. Model 1116 card recorder; weekly, 2 color record; clock driven; fully automatic. (c.1928) Value: $500.

Simplex (Wall Model), manufactured by the Simplex Time Recorder Company, Gardner, Massachusetts (formerly the W.H. Bundy Time Recorder Company). Sheet recorder model, 30 employees. (c.1925) Value: $800.

Simplex (Wall Model), manufactured by the Simplex Time Recorder Company, Gardner, Massachusetts (formerly the W.H. Bundy Time Recorder Company). Sheet recorder model, 100 employees. (c.1925) Value: $800.

Simplex (Wall Model), manufactured by the Simplex Time Recorder Company, Gardner, Massachusetts (formerly the W.H. Bundy Time Recorder Company). Serial Number: 4,421, Style 710. (c.1928) Value: $300.

Simplex Time Clock (Desk or Counter Type), manufactured by the Simplex Time Recorder Company of Gardner, Massachusetts (formerly the W.H. Bundy Time Recorder Company). (c.1940) Value: $45.

# TOY TYPEWRITERS

American Flyer, manufactured by the American Flyer Manufacturing Company, Chicago, Illinois. Patent No. 1,907,379. (c.1934) Value: $35.

IBM, manufactured by "Mar Toys," Louis Marx & Company, Inc., 200 Fifth Avenue, New York, New York. Value: $35.

Junior, manufactured by Louis Marx & Company, Inc., 200 Fifth Avenue, New York, New York. Value: $25.

Junior, GSN. German.
(c.1925) Value: $150.

Petite Typewriter, made in
England by Petite
Typewriter of Nottingham.
Patents applied for. It was a
very realistic and working
typewriter for a toy.
Value: $40.

Mouseketeers, Mickey Mouse Club,
manufactured by T. Cohn, Inc., Brooklyn, New
York. Value: $25.

Practical No. 1(a) (on the right) with wood base. Practical No. 1(b) (on the left) with cast iron base. First patent: August 30, 1892; last patent: March 25, 1902. Value respectively: $50 and $75.

Souvenir Simplex, manufactured by the Simplex Typewriter Company, 644 First Avenue, New York, New York. Shown with a picture of Thomas Jefferson and Napoléon Bonaparte as well as the dates 1803 to 1903 to commemorate the 100th anniversary of the Louisiana Purchase. Value: $250.

Simplex No. 1, Special 1908, manufactured by the Simplex Typewriter Company, New York. Last patent: March 25, 1902. Value: $50.

Simplex Special No. 1, manufactured by the Simplex Typewriter Company, New York. United States patent numbers: 481,855; 621,628; 696,304; 781,473; and 1,138,427. Value: $45.

Simplex Special A35 Keyboard Model, manufactured by the Simplex Typewriter Company, New York. Last United States patent: 1,957,373. Value: $35.

Simplex Special C35 Keyboard Model, manufactured by the Simplex Typewriter Company, New York. Value: $35.

Simplex No. 100, manufactured by the Simplex Typewriter Company, New York. Last United States patent: 1,138,427. Value: $40.

Simplex No. 200, manufactured by the Simplex Typewriter Company, New York. Value: $35.

Simplex No. 300, manufactured by the Simplex Typewriter Company, New York. Last patent: 1,138,427. Value: $35.

Above:
Simplex Special Demonstrator Model A,
manufactured by the Simplex Typewriter
Company, New York. Last patent: 1,521,405.
Value: $45.

Right:
Simplex Special Demonstrator Model F,
manufactured by the Simplex Typewriter
Company, New York. Last patent: 1,521,408.
Value: $45.

Below left:
Simplex Portable Special Demonstration
Model T. manufactured by the Simplex
Typewriter Company. New York. Value: $35.

Below right:
Toyriter, manufactured by the Wayne Toy
Manufacturing Company, Dayton, Ohio.
Patent applied for. Value: $200.

Typatune, manufactured by the Electronic
Corporation of America, New York. (c.1930)
Value: $150.

Unique Typewriter, manufactured by the Unique
Art Manufacturing Company, Inc., 200 Waverly
Avenue, Newark, New Jersey. Value: $25.

Winnie-the-Pooh typewriter, manufactured by the
Tomy Company, Hong Kong. (c.1977) Value: $10.

# CHAPTER IX
# TYPEWRITERS

An Englishman, Henry Mill, was awarded a British Patent in 1714 for a device that would "impress letters on paper one after another." This was the first patented idea of the "typewriter." Unfortunately, nothing but this "record" survived. No machine, drawing, or sketch has been found.

Between 1714 and 1868, there were over 100 patents recorded for typewriters. None were especially successful. The primary reason was that none of these inventions had the ability to type substantially faster than a human could write longhand. The record for longhand production was 30 words per minute (*The Wonderful Writing Machine*, Bruce Bliven, Jr. Random House 1954.) Speed was important at the time. Faster was better because it could potentially increase an individual's productivity. Speed could save time.

In 1868, two Milwaukee, Wisconsin residents, Christopher Latham Sholes and Carlos Glidden, were granted their first patent for a typewriter.

Sholes & Glidden, first practical typewriter

In 1873, Sholes and his partners persuaded an Ilion, New York firearms manufacturer, E. Remington & Sons, to produce their typewriter. Their first direct mail advertising claimed that their new Sholes & Glidden typewriter was capable of typing two to three times as fast as the pen. Therefore, one person could do the work of two. This was the selling point that caused the success of the Sholes & Glidden. It is also the reason why Remington, over the years, claimed that their machine was the "first practical typewriter" and why Christopher Latham Sholes is considered the "Father of the Typewriter."

The keyboard on this typewriter was arranged by Sholes and James Densmore, who was one of the investors and, subsequently, a partner in the venture. He was later involved in another typewriter called the "Caligraph." Sholes was the former editor of the "Wisconsin Enquirer" and, later, of the "Kenosha Telegraph." This previous experience in the typesetting industry was instrumental in the original arrangement of the keys. The keyboard developed is shown below in Remington's first catalog, which was distributed at the Centennial.

A problem developed in the placement of the characters on the keyboard. When attempting to type faster, the keys would jam. After a great deal of trial and error, Sholes & Densmore developed a keyboard arrangement to separate the most commonly used characters to allow for the typing mechanism to avoid jamming. That keyboard arrangement was later referred to as the "QWERTY" for the first five character keys on the top row of the keyboard. Once an operator was trained on this keyboard, it was next to impossible to un-train them. So the "QWERTY" keyboard remains with us today on almost all computers.

Christopher Latham Sholes, "Father of the Typewriter"

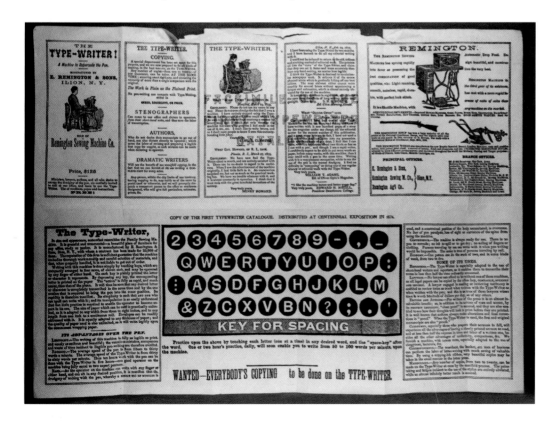

QWERTY Keyboard, developed by Sholes

147

Addressograph, manufactured by the Addressograph Company, Chicago, Illinois. An electric typing device used to emboss metal plates with names and addresses. In turn these were used to produce mailing labels at a speed from 1,000 to 10,000 impressions per hour. Serial Number: 1,289. (c.1927) Value: $400.

Adler No. 7, manufactured by Adlerwerke.vorn in Frankfort, Germany, and based on the American patents of Wellington P. Kidder. It had a forward thrust-type action as opposed to the conventional down stroke. Serial Number: 254,809. (c.1898) Value: $125.

American Visible, manufactured by the American Typewriter Company, New York, New York. An index-type action in which the operator moved a selector device to the desired letter. Serial Number: 4,183 (c.1891) Value: $1,000.

American No. 7 (type bar version), manufactured by the American Typewriter Company, New York, New York. The American had only three rows of keys and less than 350 parts. The key tops, type bars and type face were all one piece. Serial Number: 17,033 (c.1899) Value: $400.

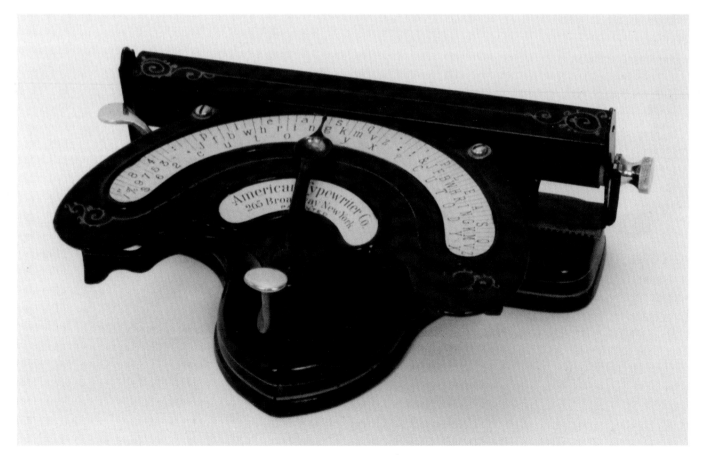

American (indicator type), manufactured by the American Typewriter Company, New York, New York. Originally sold for $10 and as a result many were purchased and are still to be found at antique markets today. (c.1893) Value: $300.

Annell' Model 3A, manufactured by the Woodstock Typewriter Company, Woodstock, Illinois. Serial Number: 1,789 (c.1922) Value: $225.

Auto Typist, manufactured by the American Automatic Typewriter Company, Chicago, Illinois. The Auto Typist was a repetitive letter writing machine with the letter stored on a pneumatic drum similar to that on a player piano. Serial Number: 019. (c.1932) Value: $500.

Barloc No. 4, manufactured by the Columbia Typewriter Company, New York. The Barloc uses a double keyboard and has type that stands straight up in a semi-circle in front of the platen and strikes straight down. It has a beautiful ornamental copper shield on the front of the typewriter. Serial Number: 10,281 (c.1893) Value: $1,600.

Bennett, manufactured by the Bennett Typewriter Company, Harrisburg, Pennsylvania. Based on today's standards, the Bennett would be called a "notebook portable." It was very compact. Serial Number: 20,576. (c.1910) Value: $250.

Bing No. 1, manufactured by Bingwerke A.G. in Germany. A compact portable fabricated in a manner similar to many toy products of that period. The No. 1 used a felt pad or roller to ink the type and is more difficult to find than the No. 2. (c.1920) Value: $350.

Bing No. 2, manufactured by Bingwerke A.G. in Germany. The No. 2 used a more conventional fabric ribbon and is more common than the No. 1. Value: $150.

152

Caligraph No. 1, manufactured by the American Writing Machine Company, New York. The second successful typewriter to appear on the American market. It had a separate key for every character. (c.1882) Value: $5,000.

Cash Typograph, manufactured by the Typograph Company.
A flat bed, down stroke machine designed to type on heavy
paper or card stock. Rare. (c.1897) Value: $10,000+.

Crandall, New Model with mother-of-pearl finish, manufactured by the Crandall Typewriter Company, Syracuse, New York. Patented in 1879. Serial Number: 5,562. Value: $5,000+.

Daugherty Visible, manufactured by the Daugherty
Typewriter Company, Kittanning, Pennsylvania. By
releasing a lever on each side of the machine, both the
type and keys are easily removed. Serial Number: 3,148.
(c.1890) Value: $800.

Densmore No. 1, manufactured by the Densmore
Typewriter Company, New York, New York. Serial
Number: 1,160. (c.1891) Value: $500.

Elliott-Fisher, manufactured by the Elliott Fisher Company, Harrisburg, Pennsylvania. The Elliott-Fisher was a down stroke action machine designed to type in ledger books for bookkeeping. Serial Number: 11,622. (c.1903) Value: $250.

Emerson No. 3, manufactured by the Emerson Typewriter Company, Kittery, Maine. Half the type and type bars were located to the left of the printing point and half were located to the right. As a key was depressed the type would swing at an oblique angle to the printing point. Serial Number: 6,166. (c.1907) Value: $500.

Empire, manufactured by the Williams Manufacturing Company of Montreal, Canada. The Canadian version of the Wellington (American) and the Adler (German). Serial Number: 17,076. (c.1895) Value: $150.

International (double keyboard), manufactured in Parish, New York and distributed by W. T. Brownridge, Boston, Massachusetts. A rare double keyboard up-stroke with a three-bank keyboard. (c.1886) Value: $12,000+.

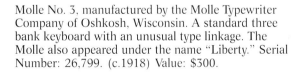

Keystone, manufactured by the Keystone Typewriter Company, Harrisburg, Pennsylvania. The Keystone used an interchangeable truss wheel for the type element. It had a three bank keyboard and double shift. Serial Number: 1,007. (c.1899) Value: $2,000.

Molle No. 3, manufactured by the Molle Typewriter Company of Oshkosh, Wisconsin. A standard three bank keyboard with an unusual type linkage. The Molle also appeared under the name "Liberty." Serial Number: 26,799. (c.1918) Value: $300.

Nippon, manufactured by the Nippon Typewriter Company, Japan. Patented by Kyoto Sugimato in 1913, the Nippon has a flat bed of 3,000 Japanese Characters. This is considered a shorthand version since the Japanese language contains in excess of 30,000 characters. (c.1959) Value: $2,500.

O'Dell No. 1b, manufactured by the O'Dell Typewriter Company, Chicago, Illinois. The O'Dell was an indicator machine that used a lineal shuttle for the type. (c.1889) Value: $1,500+.

Oliver No. 2, manufactured by the Oliver Typewriter Company, Chicago, Illinois. If there is one antique or 100 year old typewriter that every collector will have an opportunity to own, it is the Oliver. It appears frequently. The Oliver No. 1 is very rare and the Oliver No 2 is scarce, but the rest of the models are common. (c.1896) Value: $300.

Peoples, manufactured by the Garvin Machine Company, New York, New York. This indicator type machine was very popular. An inked roller inked the first model, while a later model had a conventional ribbon, which also appeared as the "Champion Typewriter." Serial Number: 5,497. (c.1896) Value: $700.

Remington 3B Portable, manufactured by the Remington Typewriter Division of Remington Rand of New York. In order to reduce parts and price, Remington developed a system of half keys. Four keys on the top row had upper and lower case numerals and most symbols were eliminated. Serial Number: C103,995 (c.1936) Value: $120.

Remington Rand Portable No. 1, This was the first new portable manufactured by Remington Rand after the purchase of the Remington Typewriter Company from Wyckoff, Seamans & Benedict. Serial Number: P 65,254. (c.1926) Value:$100.

Below:
Remington Electric, manufactured by Wyckoff, Seamans & Benedict, Ilion, New York. This was Remington's first electric typewriter. It had electrified keys and carriage movement. Only a few thousand were actually built, so it is considered to be difficult to find. Serial Number: X1,740. (c.1925) Value: $1,000.

Royal No. 1, manufactured by the Royal Typewriter Company, New York, New York. Serial Number: 76,063. (c.1906) Value: $300.

Below:
Yetman, manufactured by the Yetman Transmitter Company, New York. This was one of the first communicating typewriters. It converted Morse code to English and vice versa. The principal behind it was that you no longer needed a skilled telegraph operator to send and receive telegraph messages. Rare. Serial Number: 677. (c.1907) Value: $5,000.

# CHAPTER X
# RIBBON TINS

The typewriter, adding, calculator and cash register Industries used various means to place ink between the type mechanism and paper. Manufacturers used inkpads, ink rollers and ribbons. The ribbons seemed to be the most desirable and therefore became the inking method of choice throughout the years.

Changing a ribbon could be a very messy project. Since the ink was wet, ribbons were distributed in tiny tin containers. Each container appropriately advertising the manufacturer on the outside.

It was soon discovered that more profit was made through the ribbon replacement business throughout the life of the machine than on the initial sale of the typewriter. As a result, the market became crowded with manufacturers and competition was fierce. All kinds of variations in size, shape, and artwork on the tins were developed. There are literally thousands of variations and they can be found in almost any antique market place.

It is no wonder that collecting ribbon tins has become so popular in recent years. They are small and consequently a lot of space is not needed to house a respectable collection. They are usually inexpensive and on any given antique field trip, you are likely to find a ribbon tin you do not have. It can be a lot of fun and some more serious ribbon tin collectors have accumulated over thousands of variations.

Some manufacturers sold serial numbered "coupon books" at the time of the machine sale. In this way a customer could get a quantity price discount, but not have to store the ribbons and run the risk of unused ribbons drying out and becoming useless. Most ribbons had a shelf life printed in code on the outside of the container, after which the ink dried out and no longer could print a legible character.

Ribbons came in cotton, nylon, silk and banlon. A later variation was the carbon paper ribbon, made with a dry process that created a sharp, crisp impression with no ink spatter on the paper as was experienced with wet ribbons. This type of ribbon could only be used once.

The pricing of ribbon tins is based upon the availability of a particular tin, the uniqueness of the artwork, and, finally, it's condition. In most cases, the ribbon tins that follow show the exact price paid by the author.

American Visible, manufactured by the American Numbering Machine Company, Brooklyn, New York. Dimensions: 1.68" x 1.68" x .38". Value: $35.

American Brand, manufactured by Hess Hawkins Company, Brooklyn, New York. Dimensions: 2.50" x 2.50" x .75". Value: $12.

Bates Stapler, Wire Spool Refill, manufactured by Bates Manufacturing Company, Orange, New Jersey. Dimensions: 1.75" x 1.75" x .75". Value: $15.

Battleship (large tin with newer ship), manufactured by F.S. Webster Company, Boston, Massachusetts. Dimensions: 2.50" x 2.50" x .75". Value: $15.

Battleship (small tin), manufactured by the F.S. Webster Company, Boston, Massachusetts. Dimensions: 2" x 2" x .75". Value: $15.

Beaver Superb Ribbon, manufactured by M.D. Cook Company, Chicago Illinois. Dimensions: 2.50' x 2.50" x .75". Value: $15.

Battleship (large tin with older ship), manufactured by F.S. Webster Company, Boston, Massachusetts. Dimensions: 2.50" x 2.50" x .75". Value: $25.

Bucki Supreme, manufactured by the Buckeye Ribbon and Carbon Company, Cleveland, Ohio. (back view) Dimensions: 2.50" x 2.50" x .75". Value: $8.

Bucki Supreme (front view)

Burroughs Mainline, manufactured by Burroughs, Incorporated, Detroit, Michigan. Dimensions: 2.625" diameter x .75". Value: $4.

Burroughs Typewriter Ribbon, manufactured by Burroughs Adding Machine Company, Detroit, Michigan. Dimensions: 2.50" diameter x .75". Value: $5.

Bundy, manufactured by Bundy Typewriter Company, Philadelphia, Pennsylvania. Dimensions: 2.50" x .75". Value: $15.

Carnation, manufactured by Miller-Bryant-
Pierce Company, Aurora, Illinois. Dimensions:
2.625" diameter x .75". Value: $15.

Colonial, Dimensions: 2.75" diameter x .75". Value: $8.

Carter's Midnight, manufactured by the Carters Ink Company,
Boston, Massachusetts. Dimensions: 2.50' diameter x .75".
Value: $8.

Dalton, manufactured by Remington Rand, Incorporated.
Dalton Adding Machine Ribbon. Patent March 15, 1915.
Dimensions: 2.25" x 2.25" x .75". Value: $35.

Decker, C.F., manufactured by C.F. Decker,
Incorporated, Philadelphia, Pennsylvania.
Dimensions: 2.50" x 2.50" x .75". Value: $10.

Dur-Edge Silk, manufactured by Remington Rand, Division of
Sperry Rand Corporation, Middletown, Connecticut.
Dimensions: 2.625" diameter x 1". Value: $12.

Dur-Edge, manufactured by Remington Rand, Division of
Sperry Rand Corporation, Middletown, Connecticut.
Dimensions: 2.68" diameter x 1". Value: $10.

Dur-Edge Silk, manufactured by Remington Rand, Division of
Sperry Rand Corporation, Middletown, Connecticut.
Dimensions: 2.50" x .50" x 1". Value: $8.

Elk Miller Line, manufactured by the Miller-Bryant-Pierce Company, Aurora, Illinois. Dimensions: 2.625" x 2.625" x .75". Value: $8.

Elk Miller Line, manufactured by the Miller-Bryant-Pierce Company, Aurora, Illinois. Dimensions: 2.625" x 2.625" x .75". Value: $4.

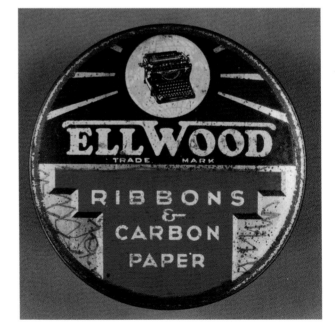

Ellwood, manufactured by Underwood Elliott Fisher Company. Dimensions: 2.25" diameter x .625". Value: $12.

Eureka, manufactured by Mittage & Volger, Parkridge, New Jersey. Dimensions: 5.50" x 7" x 2". Held one dozen ribbons. Value: $180.

Fine Service Brand, manufactured by the Steno Ribbon and Carbon Manufacturing Company, Portland, Oregon. Dimensions: 2.625" x 2.625 x .78". Value: $7.

Benjamin Franklin Brand, manufactured by Franklin Ribbon and Carbon Company, New York, New York. Dimensions: 2.625" diameter x .75". Value: $20.

Hazel Brand, manufactured by Greylock Ribbon and Carbon Company, New York, New York. Dimensions: 2.50" x 2.50" x .75". Value: $10.

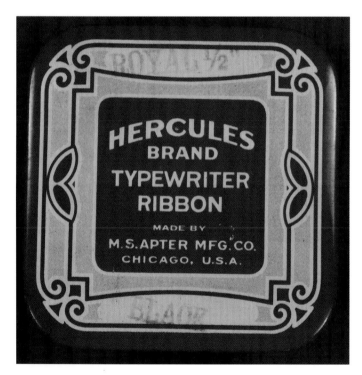

Hercules Brand, manufactured by M.S. Apter Manufacturing Company, Chicago, Illinois. Dimensions: 2.50" x 2.50" x .75". Value: $15.

Hub Brand, manufactured by F. S. Webster Company, Boston, Massachusetts. Dimensions: 2" x 2" x .75". Value: $12.

International, manufactured by Electric Writing Machine Division of International Business Machines, Rochester, New York. Dimensions: 2.50" diameter x .75". Value: $10.

Invincible, manufactured by American Writing Machine Company, New York, New York. Dimensions: 2.50" diameter x .75". Value: $20.

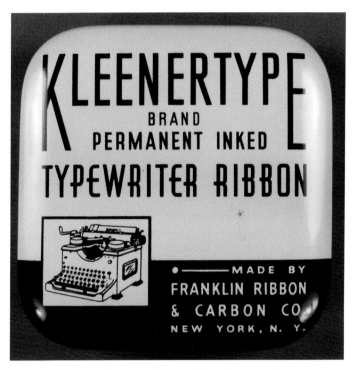

Kleenertype, manufactured by Franklin Ribbon and Carbon Company, New York, New York. Dimensions: 2.625" x 2.625" x .75". Value: $10.

Invincible, manufactured by Remington Rand, Division of Sperry Rand Corporation, Middletown, Connecticut. Dimensions: 2.75" diameter x 1". Value: $12.

Kolograph, manufactured by the W.H. Preece & Company, LTD., Manchester, England. Dimensions: 2.50" x 2.50" x 1". Value: $35.

L C Smith, manufactured by John Underwood and Company, New York, New York. Dimensions: 2.50" x 2.50" x .75". Value: $15.

Liberty, manufactured by Liberty Typewriter Company, Philadelphia, Pennsylvania. Dimensions: 2.50" x 2.50" x .75". Value: $10.

Little's Indeliba, manufactured by A.P. Little, Incorporated, Rochester, New York. Dimensions: 2.50" diameter by .875". Value: $15.

McGregor, manufactured by McGregor Incorporated, Washington, D.C. Dimensions: 2.625" diameter x .875". Value: $8.

Milo, manufactured by Milo Ribbon and Carbon Corporation, Pennyan, New York. Venus diMilo pictured on top. Dimensions: 2.50" x 2.50" x .750". Value: $18.

Norta Type Cleaning, manufactured by Norta Distributing Company, New York, New York. Dimensions: 1.50" x 2.25" x .75". Value: $8.

Norta Type Cleaning, manufactured by Norta Distributing Company, New York, New York. Dimensions: 2.875" x 1.750" x .750". Value: $8.

Nylex, manufactured by Remington Rand, Middletown, Connecticut. Dimensions: 2.625" diameter x 1". Value: $8.

Old Town Secretarial Ribbon, manufactured by Old Town Ribbon and Carbon Company, Incorporated, Brooklyn, New York. Dimensions: 2.750" diameter x 1". Value: $25.

Oriental Butterfly, manufactured by Codo Manufacturing Corporation, Leetsdale, Pennsylvania. Dimensions: 2.625" diameter x .875". Value: $12.

Oriental Girl, manufactured by Miller-Bryant-Pierce, Division of Smith Corona, Incorporated. Dimensions: 2.50" diameter x .875". Value: $25.

Ozalid, manufactured by General Aniline & Film Corporation, Ozalid Products Division, Johnson City, New York. Dimensions: 2.625 x 2.625 x .875". Value: $12.

Paragon, manufactured by Remington Typewriter Company, New York, New York. Dimensions: 1.750" diameter x .750". Value: $20.

Paragon, manufactured by the Remington Typewriter Company, New York, New York. Dimensions: 2.25" x 2.25" x .750". Value: $55.

Paragon, manufactured by the Remington Typewriter Company, New York, New York. Dimensions: 2.50" x .750". Value: $35.

Paragon, manufactured by Remington Rand, Division of Sperry Rand Corporation. Dimensions: 2.625" diameter x 1". Value: $12.

Paragon Remtico, manufactured by Remington Rand, Inc. Dimensions 2.625" diameter x 1". Value: $8.

Paragon Remtico, manufactured by the Remington Typewriter Company, New York, New York. Dimensions: 2.25" x 2.25" x .625". Value: $55.

Philco, manufactured by Phillips Ribbon and Carbon Company, Rochester, New York. Value: $8.

Pigeon Brand, manufactured by Corona
Typewriter Company, Incorporated, Groton,
New York. Dimensions: 1.750" x 1.750" x
.750". Value: $15.

Pilot Brand, manufactured by Chicago Manifold Products
Company, Chicago, Illinois. Dimensions: 2.625" diameter x
.750". Value: $20.

Pioneer, manufactured by Crown Ribbon and Carbon
Manufacturing Company, Rochester, New York. Dimensions:
2.50" diameter x .750". Value: $12.

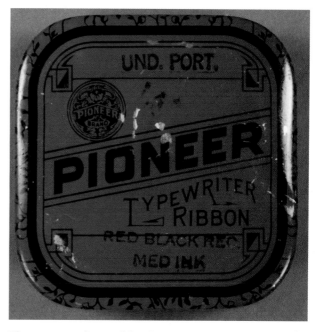

Pioneer, manufactured by the Crown Ribbon and Carbon
Manufacturing Company, Rochester, New York.
Dimensions: 2.25" x 2.25" x.750". Value: $8.

Preferred, manufactured by Aetna Products Company, Hicksville, New York. Dimensions: 2.50" diameter x .875". Value: $4.

Queen Brand, manufactured by Queen Ribbon and Carbon Company, Incorporated, Brooklyn, New York. Dimensions: 2.50" x 2.50" x .750". Value: $15.

Princess Brand, manufactured by Frye Manufacturing Company, Des Moines, Iowa. Dimensions: 2.50" diameter x .750". Value: $8.

Rainbow, manufactured by Columbia Ribbon and Carbon Manufacturing Company, Incorporated, Glen Cove, New York. Dimensions: 2.250" diameter x .750". Value: $10.

Rainbow, manufactured by Columbia Ribbon and Carbon Company, New York, New York. Dimensions: 2.250" diameter x .750". Value: $15.

Regal Brand/Remtico, manufactured by Remington Rand, Incorporated, New York, New York. Dimensions: 2.50" diameter x .750". Value: $15.

Regal "Remtico," manufactured by Remington Typewriter Company, Incorporated, New York, New York. Dimensions: 2.50" x 2.50" x .750". Value: $25.

Left:
Remington (Blue Rectangular) Paragon, manufactured by Wyckoff, Seamans & Benedict, New York, New York. Dimensions: 1.50" x 3.50" x .50". Value: $75.

Remington (Rectangular) Paragon, manufactured by Wyckoff, Seamans & Benedict, New York, New York. Dimensions: 1.50" x 1.50" x 3.50". Value: $75.

Remington Ribbon cardboard box, manufactured by Remington Office Machines Division of Sperry Rand Corporation, Middletown, Connecticut. Dimensions: 2.50" x 2.50" x 1". Value: $8.

Remington Ribbon, manufactured by Remington Rand Office Machines Division of Sperry Rand Corporation. Dimensions: 2.50" x 2.50" x 1". Value: $10.

Remrandco, manufactured by the Remington Typewriter Division of Remington Rand, Incorporated. Copyright: 1931. Dimensions: 2.625" diameter x .875". Value: $15.

Remrandco, manufactured by Remington Rand, Middletown, Connecticut. Copyright: 1931. Dimensions: 2.750" x 1". Value: $25.

Remrandco/Remtico, manufactured by Remington Rand, Bridgeport, Connecticut. Dimensions: 2.625" x 1". Value: $12.

Remrandco Brand, manufactured by Remington Typewriter Division of Remington Rand, Incorporated. Dimensions: 2.50" diameter x .750". Value: $25.

Remtico, manufactured by Remington Typewriter Company, New York, New York. Dimensions: 2.50" x 2.50" x .750". Value: $45.

Remtico Paragon, manufactured by Remington Typewriter Company, New York, New York. Dimensions: 2" x 1.750" x 1.750". Value: $70.

Remtico Paragon, manufactured by Remington Typewriter Company, New York, New York. Dimensions: 2.50" x 2.50" x .750". Value: $75.

Revilo, manufactured by the Oliver Typewriter Company. (Revilo is Oliver spelled backwards) Dimensions: 2.50" x 2.50" x .750". Value: $75.

Ruby Necklace, manufactured by Browser and Roberts, Youngstown, Ohio. Dimensions: 2.50 diameter x .750". Value: $20.

"Satin Finish," manufactured by A. P. Little, Incorporated. (Back View) 36th Year Anniversary. Dimensions: 2.50" x 2.50" x .750". Value: $125.

Smith Premier, manufactured by the Smith Premier Typewriter Company, Syracuse, New York. Dimensions: 2" x 1.750" x 1.750". Value: $75.

Silver Brand, manufactured by Kee Lox Manufacturing Company, Rochester, New York. Dimensions: 2.25" x 2.25" x .750". Value: $5.

Stafford's Immaculate, manufactured by S.S. Stafford, Incorporated, New York and Toronto, Canada. Dimensions: 2.50" x 2.50" x .750". Value: $12.

Stenotype Ribbon,. manufactured by the Stenotype Company, Incorporated, Indianapolis, Indiana. Dimensions: 1.750" diameter x .750". Value: $15.

Standard, manufactured by Standard Typewriter Ribbon Company. Dimensions: 2.5" x 2.5" x .750". Value: $8.

Stenotype, manufactured by the Stenotype Company, Chicago, Illinois. Dimensions: 1.750" x 1.750" x .750". Value: $12.

Sundstrand (with "U" instead of a key top), manufactured by Underwood Corporation, New York, New York. Dimensions: 1.625" diameter x .875". Value: $8.

Type Bar, manufactured by L.C. Smith & Corona Typewriters, Incorporated. Dimensions: 1.750" x 1.750" x .750". Value: $10.

Underwood Corporation (with keytop), manufactured by Underwood Corporation, One Park Avenue, New York, New York. Dimensions: 2.25" diameter x .50". Value: $8.

Underwood Elliott Fisher, manufactured by Underwood Elliott Fisher Company. Dimensions: 2.25" diameter x .750". Value: $4.

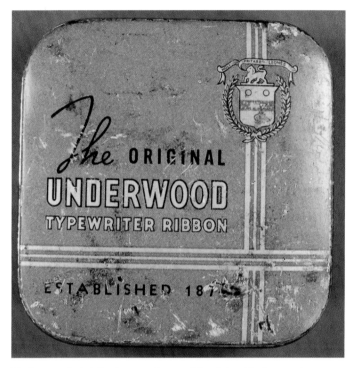

Underwood Original, manufactured by John Underwood Company with factories in Brooklyn, New York and Toronto, Canada. Dimensions: 2.50" x 2.50" x .750". Value: $20.

Underwood with type key that says Underwood Corporation, manufactured by Underwood Corporation, Burlington, New York. Dimensions: 1.50" diameter x .750". Value: $8.

USS, Dimensions: 2.50" diameter by .875". Value: $4.

U.S. Brand, manufactured by U.S. Typewriter Ribbon Manufacturing Company, of Philadelphia, Pennsylvania. Dimensions: 2.50" diameter x .875". Value: $10.

Viking Line, manufactured by Erikson Ribbon and Carbon Company, Toledo, Columbus, Cincinnati, and Cleveland, Ohio, and Detroit, Michigan. Dimensions: 2.50" x 2.50" x .750". Value: $45.

# CHAPTER XI
# EPHEMERA:
## Books, Catalogs, Correspondence, Legal Documents, Magazines and Original Patents

Most collectors of office technology are interested in related documents that provide historical information on particular inventors, manufacturers, machines or the industry as a whole.

The most commonly collected items are patents and license agreements; newspapers; magazines; reference books; biographies and letters of interest by prominent figures in the office technology industry.

An excellent example is the international office equipment magazine titled *Typewriter Topics* by the Business Equipment Publishing Company, New York, New York.

As a reference for office technologies in general, *Typewriter Topics* proves to be invaluable. The October, 1923 issue celebrated the 50th Anniversary of the typewriter Industry. That Issue refers to the beginning of the industry with the invention of the Sholes & Glidden (Remington) Typewriter in 1873. It also covers the official celebration at the Remington factory in Ilion, New York, including a speech by the then President of Remington, Harper H. Benedict, as well as reviews of the history of the Remington Typewriter. Since he was one of the pioneers of the industry, Benedict's speech is an excellent source of information for historians.

In the same issue, typewriter manufacturers and their products were reviewed. This issue of *Typewriter Topics* has been emulated several times in later years which is a testimonial to its authenticity and value.

Another American book that is a great reference on office technologies is the *Business Machine and Equipment Digest*, published by the Equipment-Research Corporation of Chicago, Illinois. The first printing was released in 1924 and is very rare. In 1928 a second issue (with updates) was released and is almost as rare.

## BOOKS

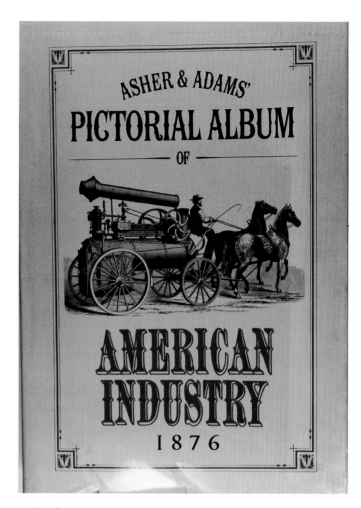

Asher & Adams. *Pictorial Album of American Industry*. 1876, New York, New York: Rutledge Books, 1976. Value: $75.

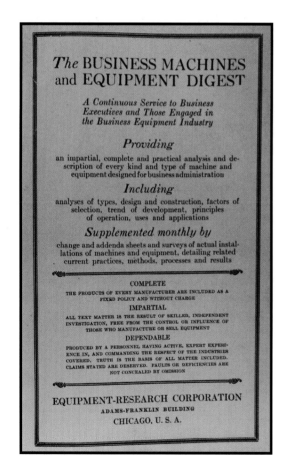

Equipment Research Corporation. *Business Machines and Equipment Digest*. Chicago, Illinois: 1928. Value: $600.

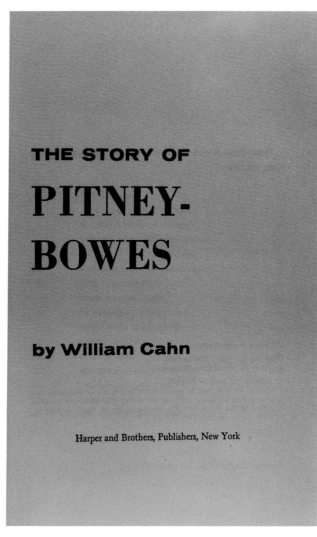

THE STORY OF

# PITNEY-BOWES

by William Cahn

Harper and Brothers, Publishers, New York

Cohn, William. *The Story of Pitney-Bowes*, New York: Harper and Brothers, 1961. Value: $25.

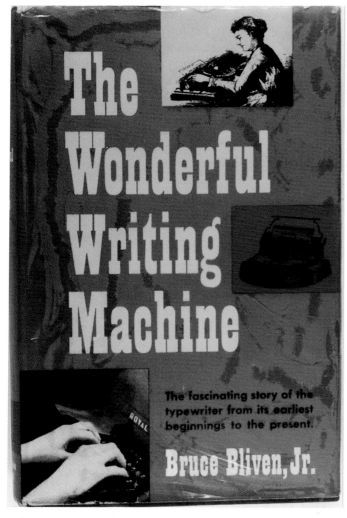

Bliven, Jr., Bruce. *The Wonderful Writing Machine*. New York: Random House, 1954. Value: $25.

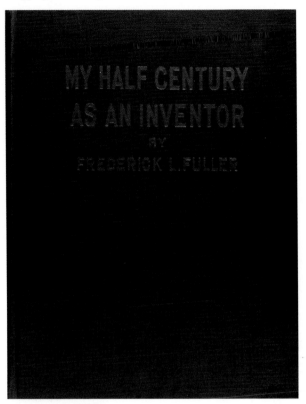

Fuller, Frederick L. *My Half Century As An Inventor*. Copyright 1938 by Frederick L. Fuller. Value: $40.

Darby, Edwin. *It All Adds Up: the Growth of Victor Comptometer Corporation*. 1968. Value: $50.

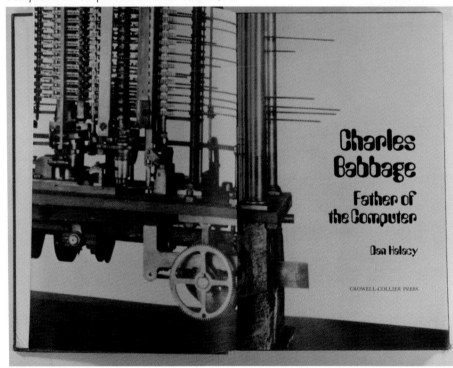

Halacy, Dan. *Charles Babbage, Father of the Computer*. New York & Toronto, Ontario: Collier-MacMillan Ltd. 1970. Value $35.

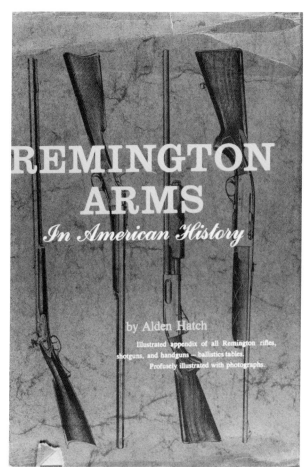

Hatch, Alden, *Remington Arms, An American History*. New York,Toronto: Rinehart & Company, Inc., 1956. Value: $35.

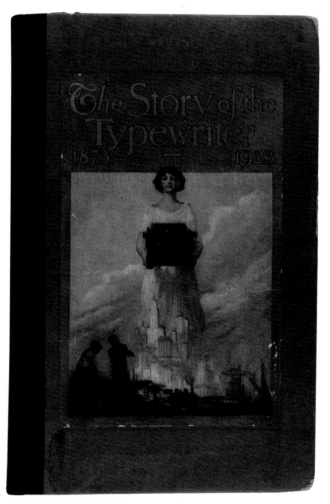

Herkimer County Historical Society. *The Story of the Typewriter: 1873-1923*. Herkimer, New York: Herkimer County Historical Society, 1923. Value: $200.

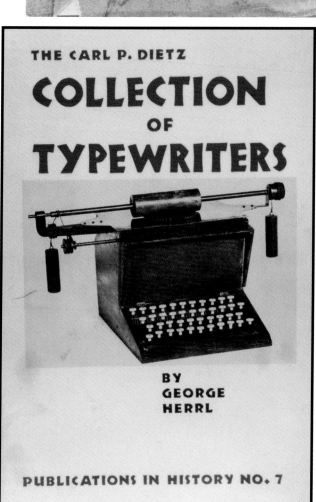

Herrl, George. *The Carl Dietz Collection of Typewriters*. Milwaukee, Wisconsin: Milwaukee Public Museum, 1965. Value: $200.

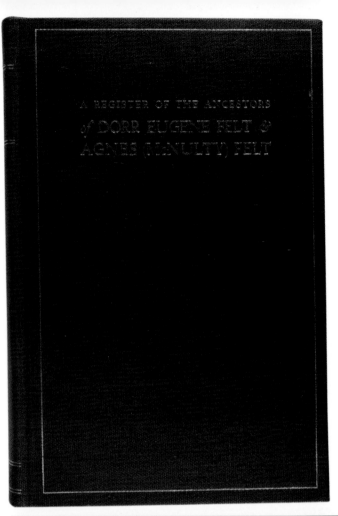

Holman, Alfred L. *Dorr Eugene Felt, and Allied Families*. Copyright, 1921. Value: $45.

Huck, Virginia. *Brand of the Tartan: the 3M Story*. New York: Appleton-Century-Crofts, Inc. 1955. Value: $25.

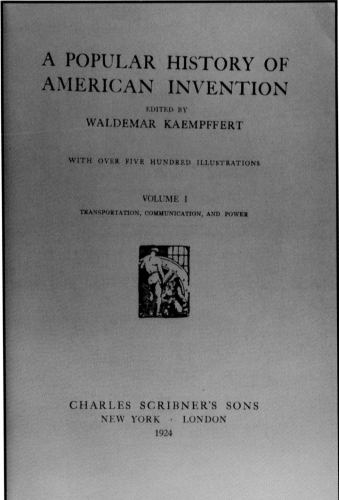

Kaempffert, Waldemar. *A Popular History of American Invention; Volumes I and II*. New York & London: Charles Scribner's Sons, 1924. Value: $55.

Marcossan, Isaac F., *Wherever Men Trade: The Romance of the Cash Register*. New York: Dodd, Mead & Company, 1948. Value: $25.

Masi, Frank T. *The Typewriter Legend*. Secaucus, New Jersey: Matsushita Electric Corporation of America, 1985. Value: $50.

Montgomerie, G.A. *Digital Calculating Machines*. London: Blackie & Son, LTD., 1956. Value: $25.

National Office Machine Dealers Association (NOMDA). *Parade of Progress*. 1985. Value: $20.

Remington Rand, Inc. *Progressive Indexing and Filing*. Buffalo, New York: Library Bureau Division, Remington Rand, Inc., 1959. Value: $25.

Rodgers, William. *Think: A Biography of the Watsons and IBM*. New York: Stein and Day, 1972. Value: $25.

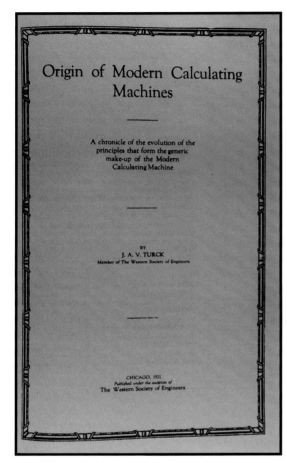

Turck, J. A. V. *Origin of Modern Calculating Machines*. New York: Arno Press, 1972. Value: $25.

Williams, Michael R. *A History of Computer Technology*. Englewood Cliffs, New Jersey: Prentice-Hall, Inc. 1985. Value: $38.

*Add-Index Combination Register and Line-A-Day System.*
Value: $25.

*The Cincinnati Time Recorder.* (c.1915) Value: $45.

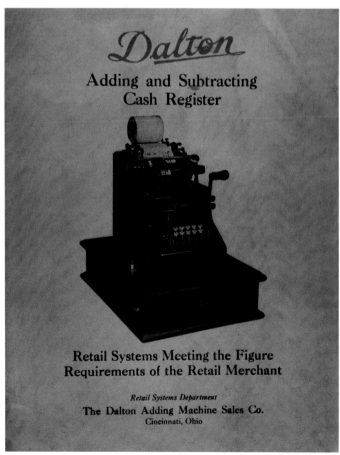

*Dalton Adding and Subtracting Cash Register.* Value: $60.

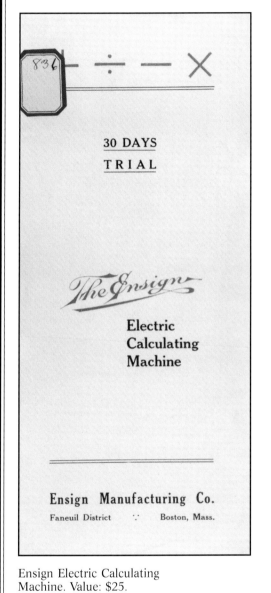

Ensign Electric Calculating
Machine. Value: $25.

Felt & Tarrant
Manufacturing
Company
instruction catalog.
Value" $65.

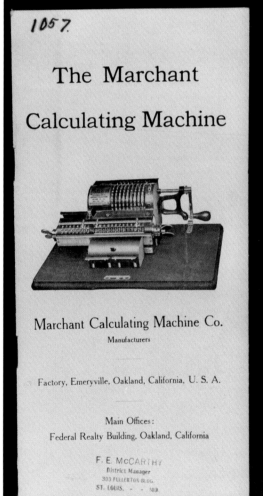

*The Marchant
Calculating
Machine.*
Value: $20.

Operator Instruction Manuals for typists. Value Each: $25-$50.

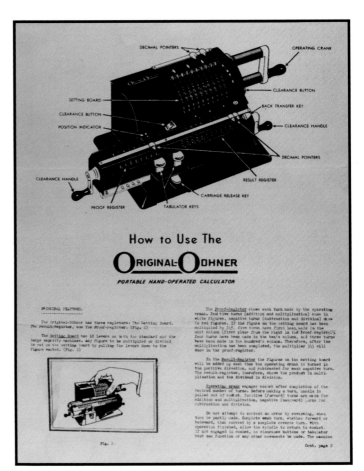

*How to use the Original Odhner.* Value: $25.

A BRIEF HISTORY
OF THE TYPEWRITER

Remington Rand, *Brief History of the Typewriter.* Value: $15.

# CORRESPONDENCE

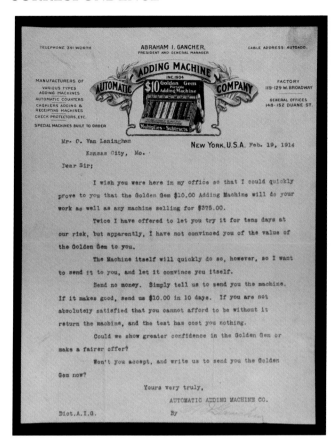

Automatic Adding Machine Company, dated February 19, 1914 and signed by President, Abraham I. Gansher. Value: $45.

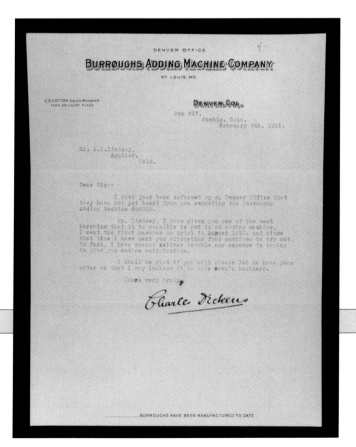

Burroughs Adding Machine Company, dated February 7, 1911. Value: $35.

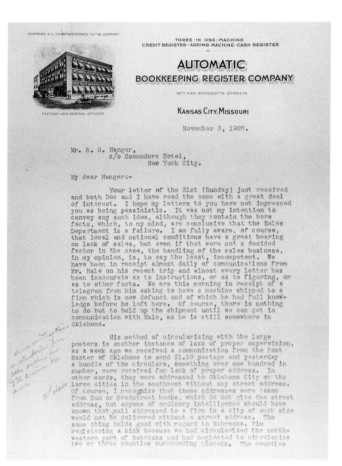

Automatic Bookkeeping Register Company, dated November 3, 1920 and signed by President Frank Laughlin. Value: $55.

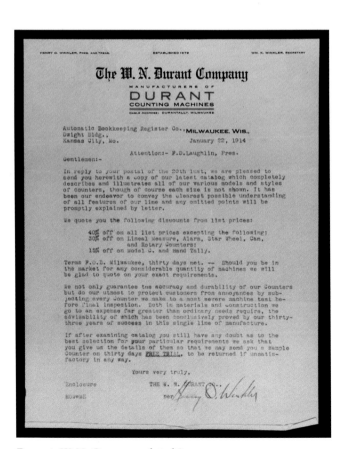

THE CALCULATOR CORPORATION

"THE CALCULATOR ADDING MACHINE"

GRAND RAPIDS, MICHIGAN, U.S.A.

Jan. 16, 1920

Calculator Corporation, dated
January 16, 1920. Value: $30.

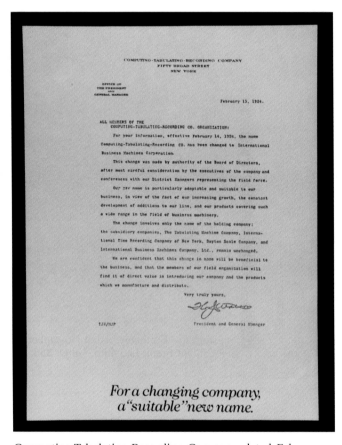

For a changing company,
a "suitable" new name.

Computing-Tabulating-Recording Company, dated February
13, 1924 and signed by their President. Value: $25.

Durant, W. N. Company, dated January
22, 1914. Value: $20.

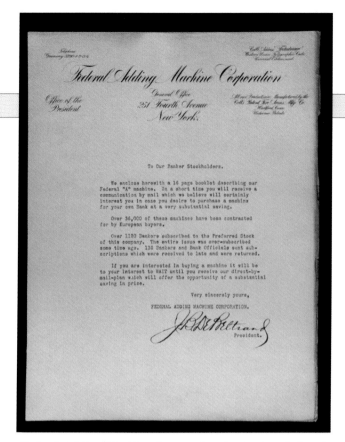

Federal Adding Machine Corporation (c.1917) and signed by their President. Value: $25.

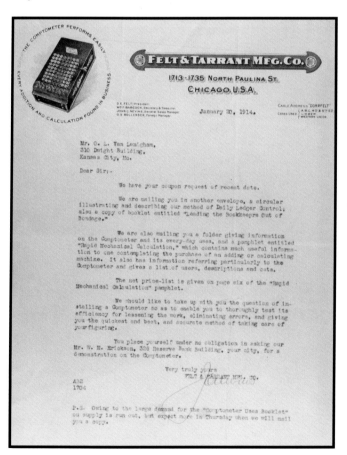

Felt & Tarrant Manufacturing Company, dated January 20, 1914. Value: $45.

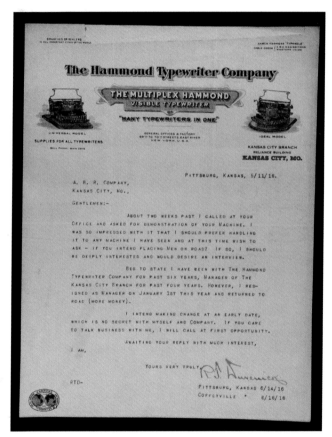

Hammond Typewriter Company, dated May 11, 1916. Letterhead displays both the Universal and Ideal Model Typewriters. Value: $55.

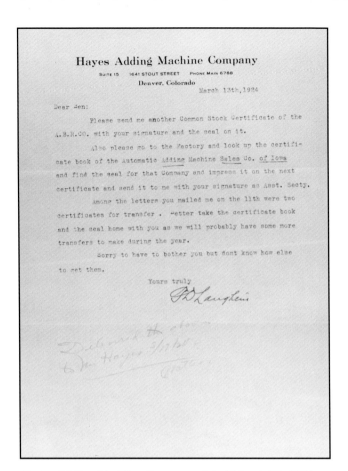

Hayes Adding Machine Company, dated March 13, 1924.
Value: $20.

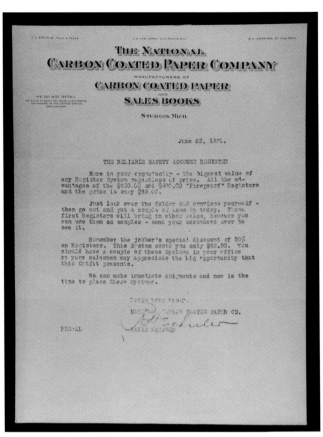

National Carbon Coated Paper Company, dated June 23, 1920. Value: $25.

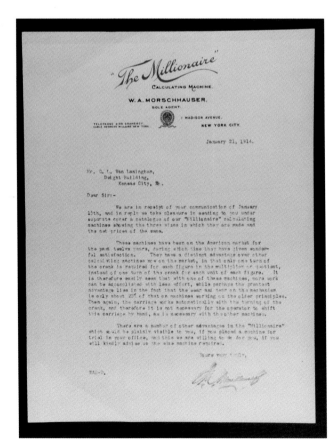

Millionaire Calculating Machine, dated January 21, 1914.
Value: $45.

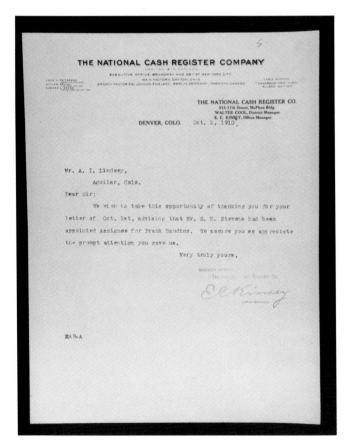

National Cash Register Company, dated October 5, 1910.
Value: $35.

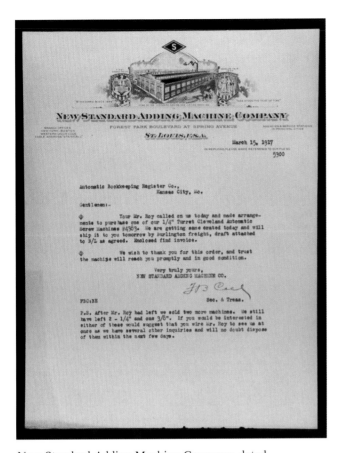

New Standard Adding Machine Company, dated
March 15, 1917. Value: $55.

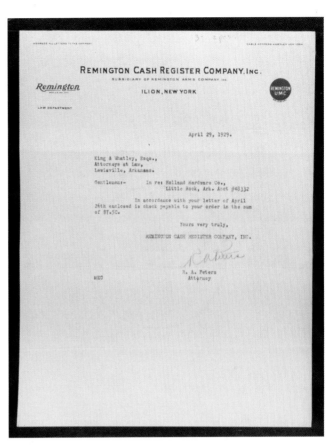

Remington Cash Register Company, Inc., dated
April 29, 1929. Value: $30.

Oliver Typewriter Company, dated February 8, 1907 with
original envelope and $.02 stamp. Value: $65.

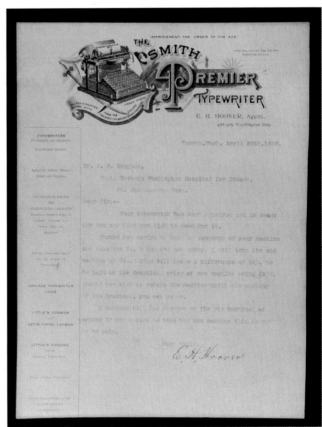

Smith Premier Typewriter Company, dated April 25,
1896 from an agent of Smith Premier. Value: $40.

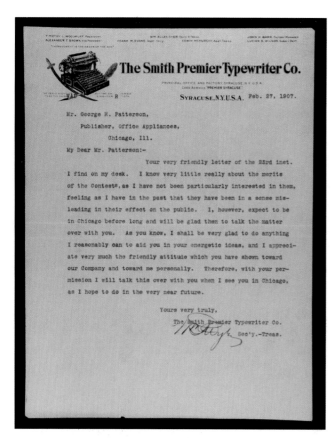

Smith Premier Typewriter Company, dated February 27, 1907, on manufacturer's letterhead. Value: $40.

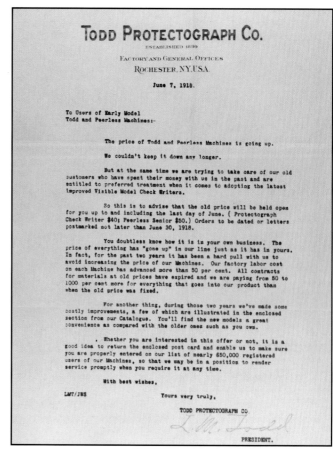

Todd Protectograph Company, dated June 7, 1918 and signed by their president. Value: $40.

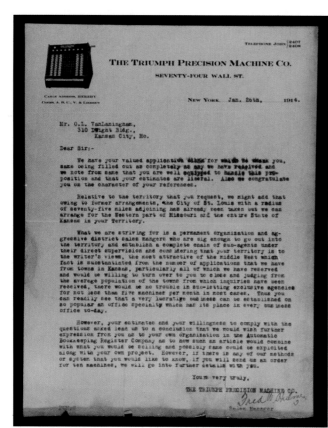

Triumph Precision Machine Company, dated January 20, 1914. Value: $55.

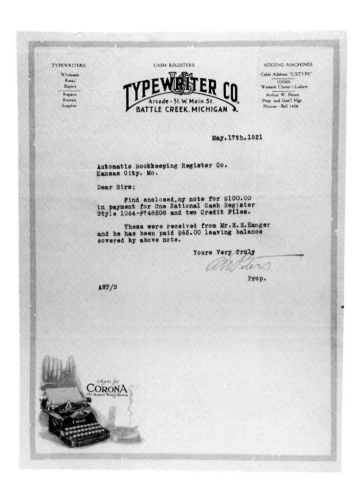

Typewriter Company, dated May 17, 1921, an agent for Corona Typewriter Company. Value: $20.

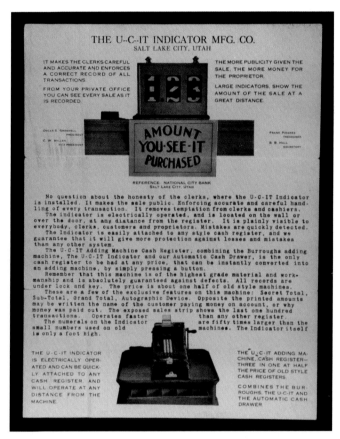

U - - C - - It Indicator Manufacturing Company. (c.1915) Value: $25.

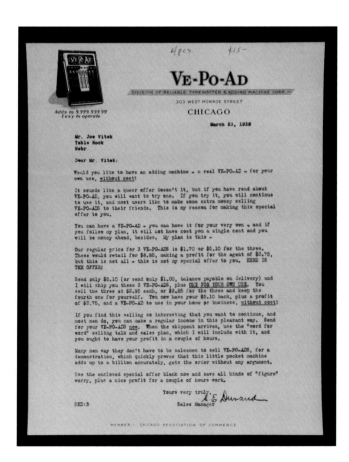

Ve-Po-Ad, a division of Reliable Typewriter and Adding Machine Corporation, dated March 23, 1939. Value: $45.

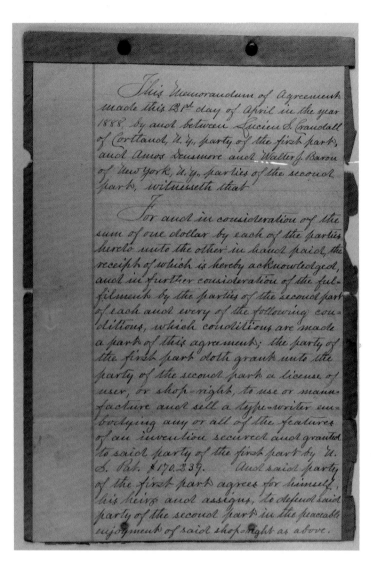

License Agreement between Lucien S. Crandall and Amos Densmore and Walter Baron dated April 21, 1888, in reference to patent number 170,239. Value: $250.

AGREEMENT made this 30th day of June A. D. 1899 between ALBERT H. ELLIS of the Borough of Manhattan, City, County and State of New York, hereinafter designated the party of the first part, and Wyckoff, Seamans & Benedict, a corporation duly organized and existing under the Laws of the State of New York, hereinafter called the party of the second part.

WHEREAS the party of the first part has made a certain invention, consisting of an Automatic Adding Attachment for typewriting machines for which an application for Letters Patent of the United States was made and filed in the United States Patent Office on the 23rd day of January 1899, Serial No. 703,055, which application has been allowed, as by reference thereto will more fully and at large appear.

WHEREAS the party of the second part is desirous of acquiring an interest in and the control of said invention, and to perfect and apply the same as an attachment to typewriting machines, and the said party of the first part is willing to assign and convey his interest in and to said invention and any improvements thereon or applicable thereto, upon the terms and conditions hereinafter sated and set forth.

NOW THEREFORE THIS AGREEMENT WITNESSETH that for and in consideration of the sum of one dollar to each in hand paid the receipt whereof is hereby acknowledged, and in consideration of the faithful performance of the covenants and agreements herein contained, the parties hereto have agreed and do hereby agree as follows:-

FIRST.- The party of the second part agrees to pay to the party of the first part the sum of $2250 in cash on the execution and delivery of this agreement; and it further agrees to employ the said party of the first part for

Agreement between Albert H. Ellis and Wyckoff, Seamans and Benedict dated June 30, 1899. The agreement covers the purchase rights to Ellis's patent number 703,055. Value: $250.

License Agreement between the Densmore Typewriter Company, Max W. Weir and Walter Baron dated January 21, 1902. Value: $240.

Letter from the Solicitor of Patents to Union Typewriter Company (C.W. Seamans) involving the Visible Writing Machine Company and Brooks. Value: $75.

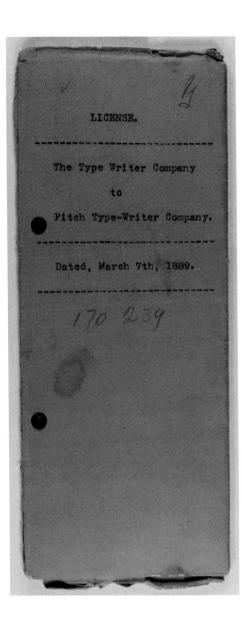

LICENSE.

- - - - - - - - - - - - - - - - - - - - -

The Type Writer Company

to

Fitch Type-Writer Company.

- - - - - - - - - - - - - - - - - - - - -

Dated, March 7th, 1889.

- - - - - - - - - - - - - - - - - - - - -

170 239

License Agreement between the Typewriter Company and the Fitch Typewriter Company, dated March 7, 1889. Value: $300.

1.

WHEREAS, Lucien S. Crandall did heretofore obtain Letters Patent of the United States for "Improvement in Type-Writing Machines", bearing date November 23rd, 1875, and numbered 170,239; and

WHEREAS, the said Crandall did thereafter assign and convey to George W.N. Yost, an equal, undivided one-half part of said Letters Patent and the inventions thereby secured, or intended so to be, which said equal, undivided one-half part, the said George W.N. Yost did afterwards assign and convey to The Type Writer Company, a corporation, under the laws of the State of New York, of which said equal, undivided one-half part of said Letters Patent and of said inventions, said The Type Writer Company is now the owner and holder; and

WHEREAS, the Remington Standard Typewriter Manufacturing Company is the exclusive licensee of said The Type Writer Company under the said equal, undivided one-half part of said Letters Patent and said inventions, so far as an exclusive license can be granted thereunder; and

WHEREAS, the Fitch Type-Writer Company, a corporation, under the laws of the State of Iowa, is desirous of obtaining a license under the said equal, undivided one-half part and is willing to pay therefor to The Type Writer Company Five Hundred Dollars, and to the Remington Standard Typewriter Manufacturing Company certain considerations embodied in a separate agreement between the said Remington Standard Typewriter Manufacturing Company and the said Fitch Type-Writer Company, to which reference is hereby made, for the consent of the said Remington Standard Typewriter Manufacturing Company to the granting of this license by said The Type Writer

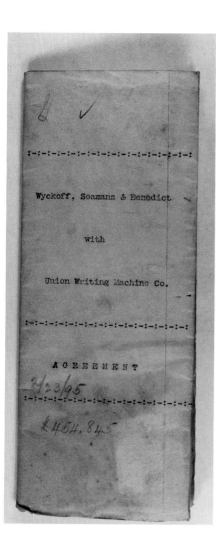

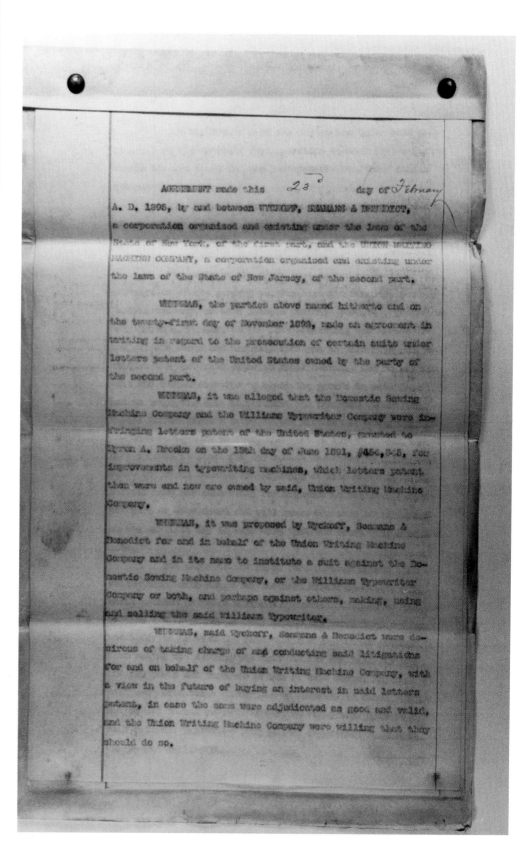

Agreement between Wyckoff, Seamans & Benedict and the Union Writing Machine Company, dated February 23, 1895. Value: $250.

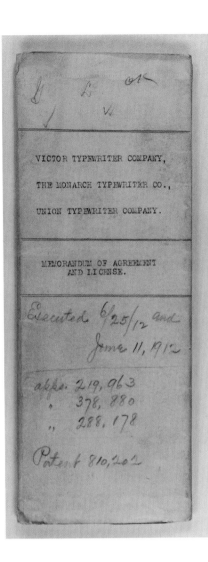

Memorandum of Agreement and License between Victor Typewriter Company, Monarch Typewriter Company and the Union Typewriter Company, dated June 25, 1912. Value: $250.

MEMORANDUM OF AGREEMENT AND LICENSE made this
day of May, 1912, by and between the Victor Typewriter Company, a corporation organized and existing under
the laws of the State of New York, party of the first part;
The Monarch Typewriter Company, a corporation organized
and existing under the laws of the State of New York, party
of the second part, and the Union Typewriter Company, a corporation organized and existing under the laws of the State
of New York, party of the third part;

WHEREAS the party of the first part is the owner
of all the right, title and interest in and to certain inventions relating to Typewriting Machines made by William
H. Hulse, and for which application for Letters Patent of
the United States was filed in the U. S. Patent Office on
July 9th, 1904, Serial No. 215,965;

And the party of the first part is also the owner
of all the right, title and interest in and to the United
States Letters Patent No. 810,202, granted January 16th,
1906, to John A. Hagerstrom, for Improvements in Typewriting
Machines, and in and to the inventions or improvements secured thereby;

AND WHEREAS the said party of the first part has,
as assignee and through said Hagerstrom, applied for a re-
issue of the said Letters Patent No. 810,202, which reis-
sue application was filed on June 13th, 1907 and bears
Serial No. 378,880;

AND WHEREAS the party of the second part is the
owner of all the right, title and interest in and to the

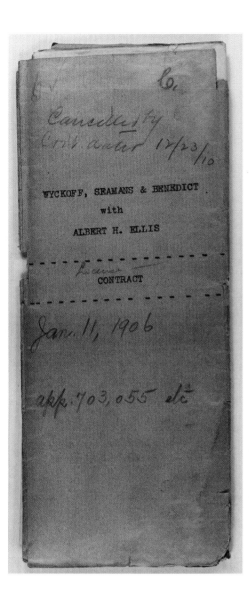

WYCKOFF, SEAMANS & BENEDICT

with

ALBERT H. ELLIS

CONTRACT

Jan. 11, 1906

app. 703,055 etc

License Agreement between Wyckoff,
Seamans & Benedict and Albert H.
Ellis, dated January 11, 1906.
Value: $250.

AGREEMENT made this 11th day of January, 1906, between ALBERT H. ELLIS, now residing at Kingston, Ulster County, New York, hereinafter called the party of the first part, and WYCKOFF, SEAMANS & BENEDICT, a corporation under the laws of the State of New York, hereinafter called the party of the second part.

WHEREAS heretofore and on the thirtieth day of June, 1899, the parties hereto entered into a written agreement, whereby the party of the first part contracted to enter the service of the party of the second part under certain conditions specified.

WHEREAS in pursuance of said agreement the party of the first part entered the service of the party of the second part, and assigned to the party of the second part his application for Letters Patent then pending in the United States Patent Office, Serial No. 703, 055, and has since been engaged in perfecting said invention and in making other improvements in automatic adding attachments for typewriting machines for which application for Letters Patent of the United States have been filed, and which inventions, improvements and applications said party of the first part has duly assigned to the party of the second part as provided in and by said agreement.

WHEREAS the party of the first part desires to amend the agreement of June 30th, 1899, and the party of the second part has consented thereto;

NOW THEREFORE, this agreement witnesseth, that for and in consideration of One dollar ($1.00), the receipt of which is hereby acknowledged, and the faithful performance of the covenants and agreements hereinafter set forth, the parties hereto have agreed, and do hereby agree as follows:

FIRST.- The party of the second part shall have until December 31, 1910 inclusive, in which to decide whether it will or will not manufacture and sell automatic adding attach-

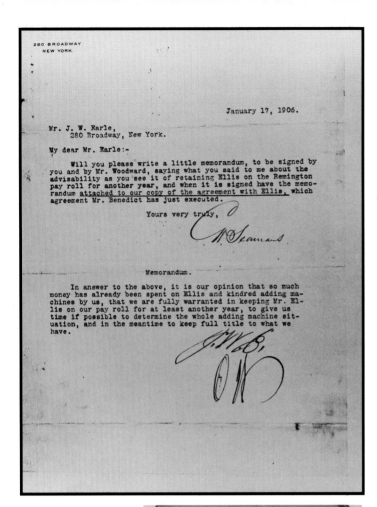

January 17, 1906.

Mr. J. W. Earle,
    280 Broadway, New York.

My dear Mr. Earle:-

    Will you please write a little memorandum, to be signed by
you and by Mr. Woodward, saying what you said to me about the
advisability as you see it of retaining Ellis on the Remington
pay roll for another year, and when it is signed have the memorandum attached to our copy of the agreement with Ellis, which
agreement Mr. Benedict has just executed.

    Yours very truly,

    Memorandum.

    In answer to the above, it is our opinion that so much
money has already been spent on Ellis and kindred adding machines by us, that we are fully warranted in keeping Mr. Ellis on our pay roll for at least another year, to give us
time if possible to determine the whole adding machine sit-
uation, and in the meantime to keep full title to what we
have.

Letter regarding the employment of A.H. Ellis and his remaining on the Remington payroll for one additional year, dated January 17, 1906. Value: $35.

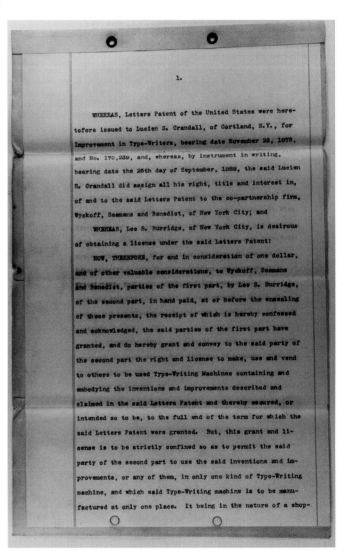

Left and above:
License Agreement between Lee S. Burridge and Wyckoff, Seamans & Benedict, dated October 13, 1888, pertaining to the Crandall patent number 170,239. Value: $250.

*Scientific American*, Volume XXVIII, No. 6, New York, dated August 10, 1872. Article on early Sholes Typewriter. Value: $75.

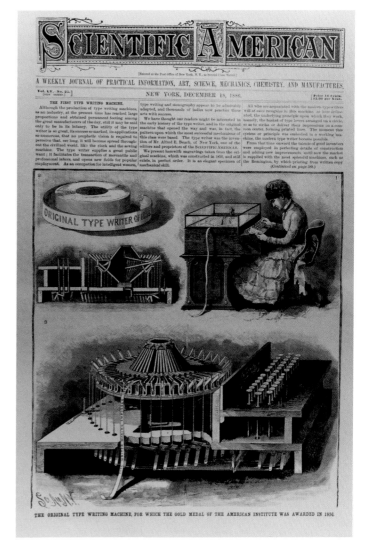

*Scientific American*, Volume LV, No. 25, New York, dated December 18, 1886. Article on first writing machine, 1856, invented by Alfred E. Beach a former editor and proprietor of the *Scientific American*. Value: $75.

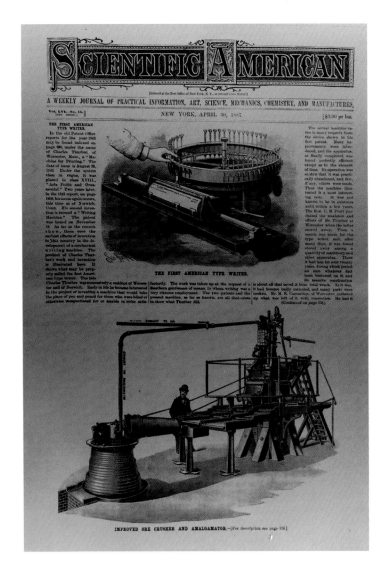

*Scientific American*, Volume LVI, No. 18, New York, dated April 30, 1887. Article on the 1843 Charles Thurber Typewriter. Value: $75.

*Scientific American*, Volume LIX, No. 24, dated December 15, 1888. Article on manufacturer of Remington typewriters. Value: $75.

*Scientific American*, page 68, dated February 3, 1894. Article on Edison typewriter. Value: $30.

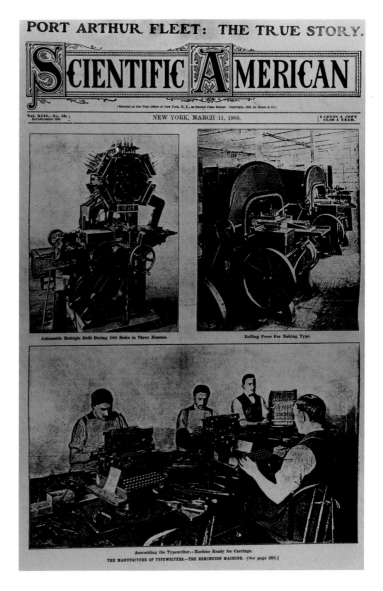

*Scientific American*, Volume XCII, New York, dated March 11, 1905. Article on the manufacture of Remington typewriters. Value: $75.

*Typewriter Topics*, Volume LV, No. 2, dated October, 1923 - the 50th Anniversary of the Typewriter issue. Value: $300.

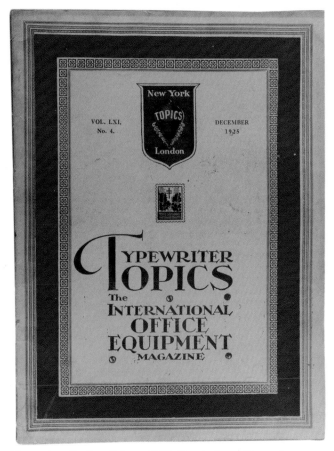

*Typewriter Topics*, Volume LXI, No. 4, dated December, 1925. Value: $125.

*The Typewriter*, Volume I, No. 1, New York, dated May, 1980. Article by G. W. N. Yost on who invented, built and bought out the Remington, Caligraph and Yost typewriters. Value: $300.

# ORIGINAL PATENTS

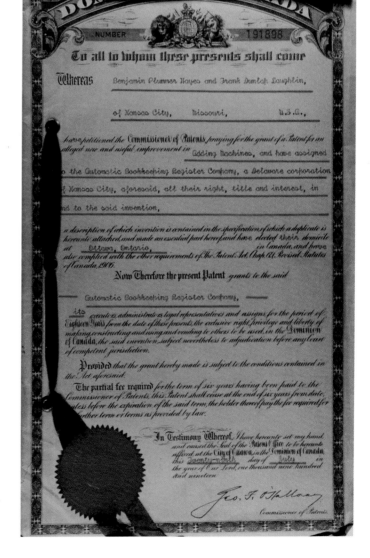

U.S. Patent Number 1,195,308, dated August 22, 1916 for Filing Cabinets invented by George White. Value: $300.

Canadian Patent Number 191,898, dated July 29, 1919 for inventors Hayes & Laughlin on Accounting Machines. Value: $300.00.

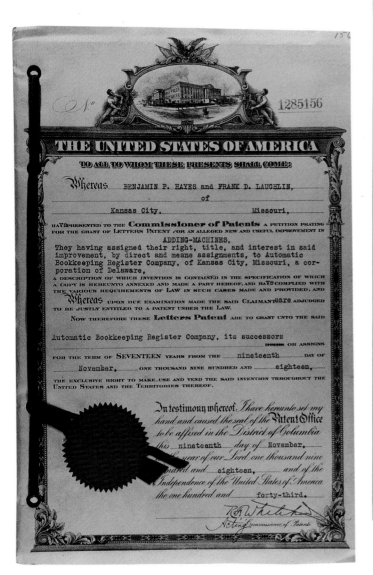

U.S. Patent Number 1,285,156, dated November 19, 1918 for inventors Hayes & Laughlin on Adding Machine. Value: $300.

U.S. Patent Number 1,362,792, dated December 21, 1920 on printer tables for Cash Registers by Benjamin Hayes. Value: $300.

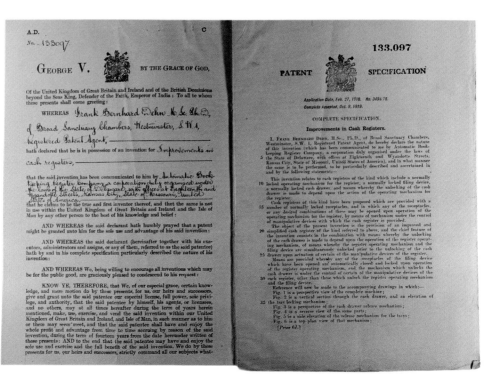

British Patent Number 133,097, dated October 9, 1919 on Cash Register for Automatic Bookkeeping Register Company. Value: $200.

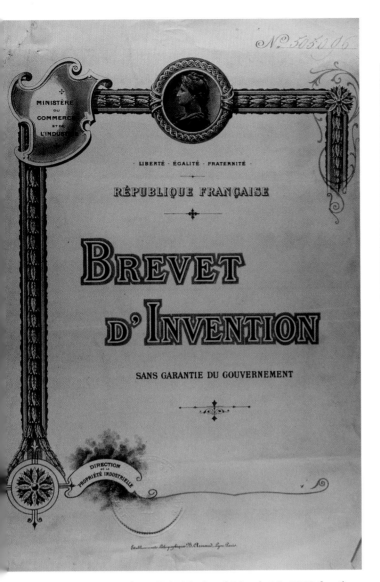

French Patent Number 505,095, dated March 18, 1918 for the Automatic Bookkeeping Register Company. Value: $200.

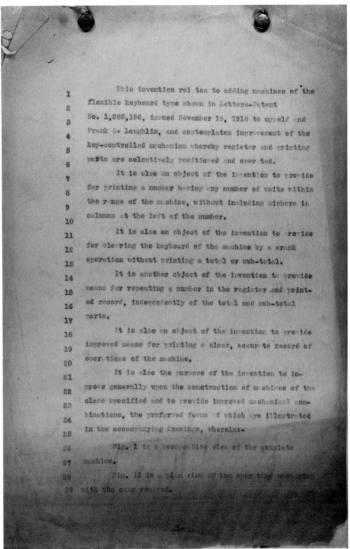

Original description draft and drawings of Benjamin Hayes Adding Machine. Includes 116 pages of text and 14 pages of drawings. Value: $500.

Assignment of Patent Number 87,950 of B. P. Hayes and F. D. Laughlin to Automatic Bookkeeping Register Company dated February 11, 1918. Value: $200.

# BIBLIOGRAPHY

Adler, Michael H. *The Writing Machine: a History of the Typewriter*. London, England: Ruskin House, 1973

Beechings, Wilfred A. *Century of the Typewriter*. London, England: William Heinemann LTD, 1974.

Blivens, Bruce Jr. *The Wonderful Writing Machine*. New York, New York: Random House, 1954

Brown, Michael A. *Antique Check Writers: A Collector's Guide from A to Z*. Philadelphia, Pennsylvania: Michael A. Brown, 1998.

Crandall, Richard L. and Robins, Samuel. *The Incorruptible Cashier*. Vestal, New York: Vestal Press Ltd.,1990.

Durant, Will. *Our Oriental Heritage: The Story of Civilization: 1*. Norwalk, Connecticut: Easton Press, 1992.

Hatch, Alden. *Remington Arms: In American History*. New York, New York & Toronto, Canada: Rinehart & Company, Inc.,1956.

Hill, Henry C. *The Wonder Book of Knowledge*. Philadelphia, Pennsylvania: John C. Winston Company, 1919.

Levin, Howard. *Information on Pencil Sharpeners*. Reseda, California, 1998.

Lippman, Paul. *American Typewriters*. Hoboken, New Jersey: Original & Copy, 1992.

Martin, Ernst. *The Calculating Machines (Die Rechenmaschinen): Their History and Development*. Los Angeles & San Francisco, California: Tomash Publishers, 1992. (Translated and edited by Peggy Aldrich Kidwell and Michael R. Williams. MIT Press, Cambridge.)

Masi, Frank T. *The Typewriter Legend*. Secaucus, New Jersey: Matsushita Electric Corporation of America, 1985

McCartney, Joseph M. *Business Machines and Equipment Digest*. Chicago, Illinois: The Equipment Research Corporation, 1928.

Muirhead, James P. *The Origin and Progress of the Mechanical Inventions of James Watt*. London, England: John Murray, Albemarle Street M.DCC.LIV.

Office, The. *A Brief History of Dictating Machines*. New York, New York: ABC Publishing, March, 1969.

Rehr, Darryl. *ETCetera: Magazine of the Early Typewriter Collectors Association–Volumes 1–47*. Los Angeles, California: Darryl Rehr, 1987–1999.

Remington Typewriter Company. *Remington Notes: Volumes 1, 2, 3, 4 & 5*. New York, New York: Remington Typewriter Company, 1906–1915.

*Scientific American*. New York, New York: Munn & Company, December 20, 1913.

Yates, JoAnne. *Control through Communications: The rise of System in American Management*. Baltimore and London: Johns Hopkins University Press, 1989.

# INDEX

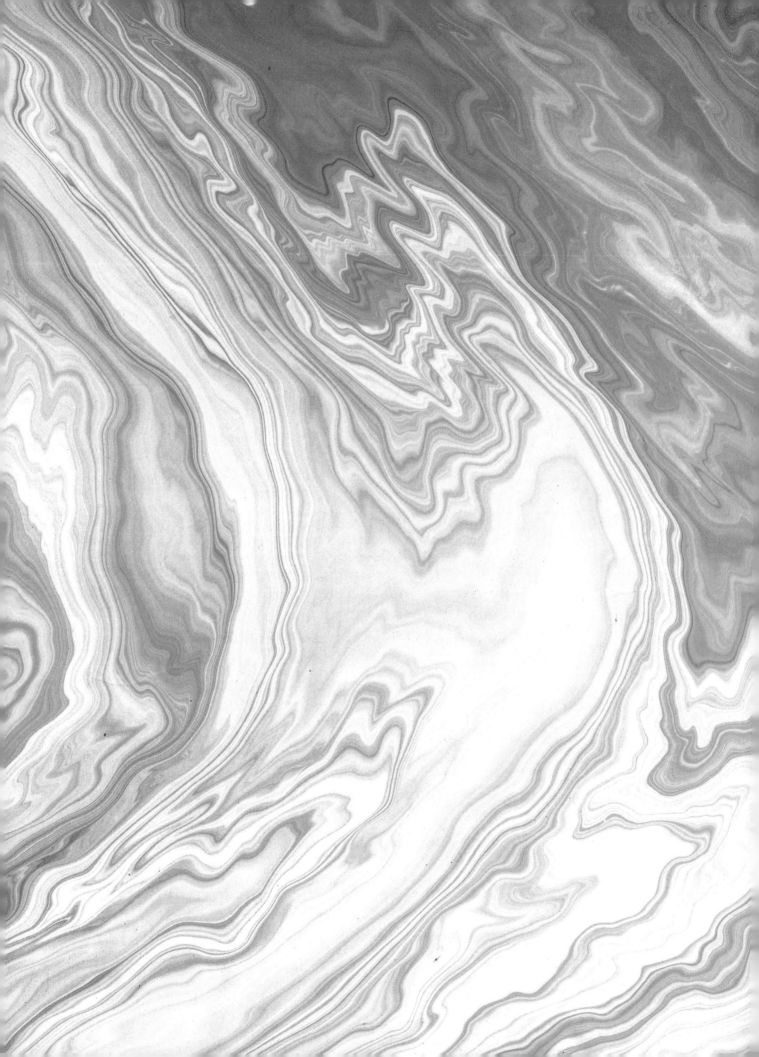